708 NEW
*
National Museum, Tokyo
SPEEDWAY P.L.   57107211

3 5550 99046324 5

D1304137

708
N

Newsweek
National museum Tokyo

WITHDRAWN
Speedway Public Library

Speedway Public Library
5633 West 25th St.
Speedway, Indiana 46224

NATIONAL MUSEUM
TOKYO

NATIONAL MUSEUM
TOKYO

Newsweek/GREAT MUSEUMS OF THE WORLD

NEW YORK, N.Y.

**GREAT MUSEUMS
OF THE WORLD**

Editorial Director—Carlo Ludovico Ragghianti
Assistant—Giuliana Nannicini
Translation and Editing—Editors of ARTNEWS

NATIONAL MUSEUM
TOKYO

Texts by:

Alberto Giuganino
Adolfo Tamburello

Design:

Fiorenzo Giorgi

Published by

NEWSWEEK, INC.
& ARNOLDO MONDADORI EDITORE

Library of Congress Catalog Card No. 68-20029

© 1968—Arnoldo Mondadori Editore—CEAM—Milan

© 1968—Photographs Copyright by Kodansha Ltd.—Tokyo

All rights reserved. Printed and bound in Italy.

THE TOKYO NATIONAL MUSEUM: FOREWORD

NAGATAKE ASANO
Director

According to our laws for the protection of national monuments, the purpose of the National Museum is to collect, preserve and exhibit works of art as well as use such works to teach. Although these are the functions of any museum, art must be seen and understood with a feeling and sensitivity which transcend the dictates of law.

There are, in the world today, museums of all types everywhere and most of them are concerned with art. But art differs from country to country. The Tokyo National Museum collects Oriental objects, principally Japanese. Our collections include nearly 90,000 objects.

Much of Oriental art cannot tolerate a long period of exposure. Paintings and calligraphy are especially delicate and must be heavily protected. The preservation of such works requires attentive and accurate care. Preservation and exhibition are two different acts and can be, by nature, contradictory. It is often difficult to find a way to reconcile both aims.

A collaboration between the part of the museum which exhibits and the part which preserves is needed, a collaboration designed for understanding what is the true meaning of holding a national treasure for posterity. He who is entrusted with the maintenance of a museum must treat the objects with reverence. The public, too, should approach the art with a sense of loving protection.

Science has helped us with the regulation of heat and humidity, with lighting and restoration techniques. But it is necessary, on the other hand, to ask ourselves if there is not also a limit to this. We cannot exclude the possibility that these methods could affect the works. Perhaps we should wait for a long period of time before we use with any degree of certainty scientific means of protection. In Japan we should not neglect the protective methods which are based on tradition and which have been proved by long experience. In any case, art works must be preserved for as long as possible in their original state.

Oriental art has specific characteristics, and we try to improve our means to serve their purpose better. Moreover, for what concerns exhibitions, we are doing our best to shed light on what are the values of our works, even though everyone has a different way of seeing beauty. Interest in the East has appreciably increased recently and at the same time Oriental art study has intensified. The activities in the Oriental sections of Western museums has become overwhelming. I think it is deplorable that Japan, a most important country in Asia, still does not have an Oriental museum as such. The Tokyo National Museum has turned its attention to this problem and has planned to build an Oriental museum in which Asiatic material of every sort would be properly displayed.

The construction of such a museum began in 1965 and work is already so far along so that it will be completed by 1968. Made of reinforced concrete, the building will

9

SPEEDWAY PUBLIC LIBRARY
SPEEDWAY, IND. 46224

have three floors and a basement, covering an area of about 3000 yards. The building will include 10 permanent exhibition halls and five special exhibition halls, as well as offices for services and administration. It will exhibit material from China, Korea, Central Asia, Southern Asia, the Pacific, India, Persia, Greece and Egypt. Presently, Chinese art, including calligraphy, painting and pottery, is preserved in our museum, but unfortunately there is no representative display of the development of these media. To get works from all these countries will be no easy task and a fundamental rule for this collection will be to integrate all the materials we already have. Yet there is no reason to hurry; good works are not easily found on the market. But when something does show up we must be careful to grab it.

Some museums have a long history behind them. I hope the Tokyo National Museum, which is almost 100 years old, can become a great world museum and that it will be dedicated to ancient Oriental art, centered on ancient Japanese art. With the help of the Japanese people, the Tokyo National Museum will become an instrument for contributing to a higher cultural level in our country. And, with that, all of humanity will enjoy a higher cultural level.

PREFACE

JO OKADA
Director of the Department of Arts and Sciences

The Tokyo National Museum developed contemporaneously with Western culture in Japan. During this century, the Museum has enlarged its holdings, improved its curatorial methods and amplified its educational programs. In name and fact, it has become one of the great museums of the world.

This volume was compiled for the purpose of presenting to the public masterpieces of painting, sculpture and calligraphy which have been chosen from the numerous Museum collections. The illustrations were chosen primarily for esthetic reasons. Since the number of reproductions is limited it will be difficult to grasp through them a comprehensive idea of the development of Japanese art. The number of Chinese works is even more limited and makes it almost impossible to suggest the evolution of Chinese art history. Nevertheless, the beauty that emerges from these masterpieces does tell a history of the growth of forms in both Japan and China. And we shall roughly outline here the role that the works play in the history of art.

The pages devoted to Japanese painting include famous religious works from the Heian period (794–1185). The Tendai and Shingon Buddhist sects flourished in this era because of their close connections with nobility, as well as the wide-spread faith in *Jodo* (Pure Earth or Paradise) and the veneration of *Hokke-kyo* (Sutra of the Lotus). These new Buddhist tendencies inspired a flourishing of religious paintings. Other works which relate to Buddhism are the great *Jigoku Zoshi* (Scroll of Hells) and *Gaki Zoshi* (Scroll of the Famished Spectres), which must be considered examples of religious works between the end of the Heian and the beginning of the Kamakura period. In that time, the philosophy of the Six Worlds was widespread. Buddhist cosmology divided the universe into six parts, the worlds of hell, ghosts, animals, Ashura, humanity and heaven. Toward the end of the Heian period Japanese nobles tired of metaphysics and craved paintings of a profane nature. Decorative panels on sliding doors (*fusuma*) and screens (*byobu*) often shone in patrician houses. Typically Japanese in style, these works were called *yamato-e* (Painting of Yamato). As the style evolved from *kara-e* to *yamato-e,* or from Chinese to Japanese styles, calligraphy, as well, became more and more Japanese. The artist Ono no Michikaze helped in this process with his *Imperial Rescript for Conferring a Posthumous Title on the Monk Enchin* (p. 79), and the Japanization was perfected by Fujiwara Yukinari with his *Scrolls of the Poetry of Po Chu-i.*

The following Kamakura period (1158–1333) is the golden age of the *emakimono,* and many masterpieces were produced. The *Heiji Monogatari Ekotoba (Illustrated Scrolls of Heiji)* and the *Ippen Shonon Eden (Illustrated Biography of the Monk Ippen),* p. 107, clearly demonstrate the typical realistic tendencies of the time. Unlike the *yamato-e,* suffused with a lyrical harmony of colors and lines, ink painting in China during the Muromachi period (1337–1573) injected the severity of Buddhist spirit into the monochromatic expression of black and white. Zen is the main

11

cultural nucleus in this period and the taste for Chinese art with Zen overtones enhances Kanga painting. The elements of ink painting in China were made known by the monks Nyosetsu and Shubun and Sesshu. The *chinso* or the portraits of Zen Patriarchs took on a major importance in the Kamakura period.

An event of the Muromachi period that cannot be overlooked is the foundation of the Japanese Kanga school, which took its name from the Chinese Kano school and for a long time enjoyed the support of the samurai.

During the Momoyama period, Kano Eitoku, founder of the Kano school (p. 122), showed a remarkable ability in large-scale painting. At that time, huge paintings for sliding doors and screens used in the decoration of palaces and castles were in great demand. Hasegawa Tohaku and Kaiho Yusho were also masters of a technique adapted to monumental works. In the Momoyama period, paintings that profiled the tranquil existence of the middle-class and samurai appeared, and they became even more important in the later Edo period (1615–1867).

In the Edo period also flourished the Sotatsu and Korin schools and the Bunjinga school ("painting of the intellectuals") as well as the continuing Kano and Tosa schools. After the Meiji Restoration, Western painting loomed large in our art world and the traditional arts of Japan came under its sway.

The Tokyo National Mueseum also owns Chinese as well as Central-Asian paintings. They are not numerous, but are of extraordinary quality. It is important to note that many of the works are doubly significant because they were introduced to Japan from China many centuries ago and were influential examples. For example, a seal with the word *"Doyu"* is impressed on the painting of *Sixth Patriarch Cutting a Bambu of Liang K'ai,* which indicates that it belonged to the Ashikaga family. From family inventories the painting can be traced from the Ashikaga to the Hideyoshi family, to the Nishi Honganji Temple; it was finally transferred to the Sakai family.

The pages illustrating Chinese painting begin with an eighth-century work, *People under a Tree* (p. 31). It was found in the Turfan excavations in Hsin-kiang. Here, too, are a bodhisattva, *Ksitigarbha,* from the T'ang period (618–906) and *Two Patriarchs Purifying Their Hearts,* mid-tenth century. From there, we go to the Southern Sung dynasty works, including a *Portrait of the Poet Li Po* (p. 45) and the *Landscape with Snow* (p. 42), both by Liang K'ai. The latter also belonged to the Ashikaga family and is considered typical of the master's best work. Other pieces from the period are the *Imaginary Voyage into the Hsiao-hsiang Region* and the *Only Fisherman on the River* (p. 46) attributed to Ma Yuan.

Yen Hui, one of the major Buddhist painters, is represented in his Yuan period and from the Ming period we have reproduced Li Tsai's *Landscape* and Lu Chi's *Flowers and Birds of the Four Seasons.*

For sculpture, we have chosen Japanese, Chinese and Central-Asian works. There are also examples of ceramics, goldsmith works, objects in wood and bamboo, lacquers and fabrics from Japan. Buddhist sculpture occupies a predominant position in Japanese art. Consequently, almost all the sculpture in the Tokyo Museum consists of works from various temples; one of the greatest is the gilt-bronze group of Horyuji, known as the *Forty-eight Buddhas*.

The history of Japanese sculpture properly begins Buddhist statuary. But before the introduction of Buddhism to Japan, the Japanese had already produced terra-cotta statuettes called haniwa and the oldest form of Japanese sculpture, the *dogu*, from the Jomon period — especially in Eastern Japan. Though the clay statuettes are confined to Eastern Japan, the haniwa did not appear in the Kinki region until the sixth century A.D. and from there spread to all areas of the island. They were particularly popular in the Kanto region.

Toward the middle of the sixth century a gilt bronze statue was offered in homage by the Korean king of Paekche. This is probably the first appearance of a Buddhist statue in Japan. The Northern Wei style, of which it was an example, prevailed in China at that time, and from then on, Japanese Buddhist sculpture was influenced by the Northern Wei. The sculptor Kuratsukuribe no Tori came under its sway and started what is known as the Tori school. Among the gilt bronze statues are some with bodies and faces of children; they are characteristic of the Nara (645–784) and Hakuho periods (645–710). From the seventh to the eighth century, Buddhist T'ang art was introduced from China to Japan and with it a realist mode of sculpture. A new style was born, a combination of idealism and factuality. Lacquer techniques, which were adaptable to a realist art, also flourished.

Under the influence of Tantric Buddhism, a tradition of wood sculpture was born in the Heian period (794–1185) and later in the same period, the classic Japanese style, whose hallmark is gracefulness, was perfected. From a technical point of view, sculptures carved from one block of wood during the early Heian period were eventually replaced by sculptures assembled from several pieces. The Kamakura period signals the end of Buddhist sculpture in a highly realistic, expressionistic finale. Unlike the realism of the Nara period, which sought an ideal beauty, this art focused on details, often grotesque, of individuals.

The development of the art of the mask is also a part of Japanese art. The oldest are the *gigaku*, and tradition has it that they were introduced into Japan in 612 by a man from Korea by the name of Mimashi. The masks of the Asuka period were summarily carved in camphor wood with a powerful simplicity while masks from the Nara period were cut out of the softer paulownia wood and are more realistic. Later in the Heian period, masks of the No theater came into vogue. They were small, 13 stylized, and have a delicate face which can be twisted with pain or wreathed in a smile of joy.

In sculpture outside Japan, there is the Yun-kang Buddha which shows the freshness of early Buddhist art and served as one of the models for Japanese sculpture of the Asuka period.

Ceramics in Japan had their fullest development after the beginning of the modern period, but their history goes back to the prehistoric Jomon time. The oldest known terra-cotta pottery, with rope designs of the Jomon type, is found all over Japan, but principally in the eastern part. Examples covered with strong curved lines in relief are found in the western part of Kanto in Chubu. The Yayoi terra cottas which came after the Jomon were initially used in only western Japan, but soon spread to the eastern regions. During this period, nomadic agricultural groups began to settle on farms and produce a pottery for practical purposes. The Yayoi pottery style, which became known as *haii no utsuwa* in the Kofun period, had a long duration. The Sue terra cottas were introduced toward the middle of the fifth century from south Korea and were based on new techniques. They were worked on a lathe and fired at high temperatures in kilns dug obliquely into the earth. Made of a hard material, they were practical for daily use and came in a wide variety of types and sizes. Among the Sue, there are a few examples which are covered with a glaze made by the falling ashes in the kiln. During the Nara period, ceramic vases with colored glazes, imitating the three-colored Chinese ceramics of the T'ang dynasty, were also made. From the end of the Heian period to the Kamakura period, the Sue terra-cotta kilns began to disappear gradually and a new type of pottery appeared — the Tokoname. The ancient Seto types were produced from the Kamakura to the Muromachi period in the area of Seto. Of two types, one was glazed with greenish yellow and the other with dark brown. In the modern period, ceramic taste and technique developed considerably. Excellent objects for tea ceremonies were produced. In Kyusushu, Korean types of pottery were made and colored porcelains were created in the Kakiemon period. Nonmura Ninsei was the first to make ceramics colored in gold and silver and Kanzan introduced other new styles. The colored Nabeshima reached their perfection in the Kyoho period.

Chinese pottery exercised a major influence on the Japanese craft. Although the oldest Chinese painted ceramics date from 2500–2000 B.C., the blue and white porcelains did not develop until the T'ang dynasty. Among the most famous porcelains were those that came from the Yueh-chou kilns and among the white ones were those that came from Hising-chou of Hopei. The most characteristic ceramics of the T'ang period are, however, the three-colored wares, adorned with green, yellow, white or blue glazes.

The Sung period is considered the golden age of Chinese ceramics. Numerous kilns were built on the mainland during the period and, through advanced techniques, vast quantities of high-quality ceramics were produced. If the T'ang dynasty ceramics have opulent curves, the Sung porcelains have a simple and sober form. Even the colors are not as lively as the three-colored T'ang vases. In most cases, the Sung works are monochromatic. During the Kamakura and Muromachi periods, Lung-chuan's blue porcelains and Chinen's tea cups were abundantly imported into Japan. Among these porcelains are the Yohen which have brilliant emerald green spots on a very black background and are hailed as masterpieces throughout the world. In Muromachi texts describing the variety of ceramics, the following passage appears: "Yohen is unequaled among the Chien porcelains. There are not many in the world. They are worth an extravagant amount of money." The blue and white porcelain vases, produced from the outset of the Yuan period, reached their maximum splendor in the first half of the fifteenth century. During the Ming dynasty, ceramics glazed in red, blue, yellow and other colors were popular as well as the so-called "ancient" glazed vases.

In Korea during the Koryo period (918–1392), blue wares, very much like the Chinese blue porcelains, were made in a refined technique.

The history of metal-work techniques in Japan begins in the Yayoi period (3000 B.C.). The *dotaku* are perhaps the first beautiful Japanese products; they are presumably indigenous to Japan and were found in only the Chokou Shik and Chubu areas. They have what is known as a "running water" decoration (*ryusuimon*). From the Kofun period come mirrors, weapons, harnesses for horses, and coins which show an advanced technique in gilding and engraving. A good example is the copper crown with monsterlike figures on page 71. During the Asuka period, goldsmiths made great progress in the manufacture of Buddhist objects. The *Kanjo-ban* of Horyuji is the masterpiece of this period. The floral decoration is the most classical in the Asuka period. This type of design originated in Egypt with lotus flowers and in Greece became a continuous decorative motive. The motif was introduced into China during the fourth century, with the spread of Buddhism from India. In the Yun-kang temple grottoes we can see decorations of this type. In the Kanjo-ban decoration the floral design appears with a perfectly-shaped figure. From the Heian period on, the goldsmith technique was often used in the construction of sacred dwellings for Tantric Buddhism, such as the Kongo-ban on page 96.

In the Muromachi period the manufacture of tea pots developed in Ashiya, Tenmyo and Kyoto. Ashiya pots have a very smooth surface with a softer and more elegant design and the Tenmyo pots have a rougher surface and are usually plain and sober in taste.

The museum is poor in Chinese bronzes. One in the collection, however, is a Yu bronze, representative of the Shang-Yin period (1300–1027 B.C.). In this piece, we see figures of monsters, a decoration that often recurs on Chinese bronzes. The Eastern Chou dynasty is responsible for the first Chinese mirrors and the Han dynasty perfected them. On page 30, we have illustrated a bronze mirror from the T'ang dynasty.

Japanese lacquer ware goes back to the Jomon period. Various techniques in workmanship and decoration from China helped improve the Japanese methods. In the Heian period many objects are decorated in *maki-e* on a lacquer background, that is, made up of figures drawn with a pen and then covered with a golden dust. Since the Japanese already used this technique in Yamato-e painting, it was easy to assimilate it into lacquer ware.

In this period, the mother-of-pearl technique, introduced from China, was also assimilated into Japan and was used with the *maki-e* technique or by itself. The *maki-e* was also employed in religious object decorations, like the Sutra boxes. In the Kamkura and Muromachi periods, decorative works showed a great freedom of taste as in the toilet, cosmetic and writing boxes.

In the Edo period, lacquer ware, like other craft works, attracted highly qualified artists among whom were Honami Koetsu and Ogata Korin. Weaving developed during the Asuka period, even though Chinese immigrants who had settled in Japan had brought weaving techniques with them earlier. Pillows and banner decorations in ribbons, embroidered *ban* and *nishiki bels,* have come down to us from the Horyuji treasure. The *nishiki* are vertical, not horizontal, and have fewer colors, small designs and little variety. The horizontal *nishiki* make their appearance in the Nara period under the influence of the T'ang culture. In weaving, tinting, embroidery, various techniques were used but the most sumptuous fabrics were the *nishiki* during the T'ang period. For tinting techniques there was the *rokechi,* the *kyokechi* made from woodcuts and the *kokechi* which employed a torsion technique. Only the *emakimono* fabrics are preserved from the Heian, Kamakura and Muromachi periods. Weaving in the modern period knew a marked vitality and produced extraordinarily luxurious works like the *kosode* that everyone wore. Unlike heavy outer clothing that had been worn until then, the *kosode* showed glimpses of body flesh.

In the Edo period, a tinting technique called *yuzen* made it possible to develop the polychrome figurative designs with a liberty that embroidery does not permit. Even through the minor arts, like weaving, we are able to grasp the history and details of Japanese culture.

CHINA

VASE WITH PAINTED DECORATION. *Neolithic Period of Yang-Shao.*
In the late Neolithic era in China (3000–2000 B.C.) the peoples who had settled in the Kansu, Shensi and Honan provinces produced a considerable amount of clay pottery for domestic and funerary use. The Swedish archeologist J. G. Anderson discovered some of the pottery on his first excavation in Western Honan in 1921 and in Kansu in 1923. The earthware is classified and named according to the particular region in which it was found. There are, for example, the vases of Yang-Shao, Pan-shan, Ma-ch'ang, Hsintien, etc. Despite their early date, the vases are esthetically sophisticated, endowed with a remarkable elegance in their geometric design and artistic inventiveness. In the Panshan types from the middle Yang-shao period (circa 2000 B.C.), form and decoration harmonize so well that the works seem to have been conceived and realized in a single moment. Our illustration shows a type where a spiral rhythmically unwinds over the upper parts of the vase, echoing the elegant shape of the vase itself. Such vases are made of a thin-walled fine clay and if they are decorated with figurative forms, usually highly stylized. The handles, small, ring-like circles, blend perfectly with the decoration and surface volume.

YU BRONZE. *Shang-Yin to Chou Period.* *p. 20*
Used in religious ceremonies in honor of divinities, ancestors or celebrated personalities, ritual bronzes figure among the most beautiful and important Chinese works. These objects usually have inscriptions on the inside which tell us for what purpose they were made and sometimes include prayers for the deceased or his progeny. They vary in shape according to their use, whether it be as containers for food or wine and water. They are usually dated from 1766 B.C. to 1027 B.C. or between the first Shang-Yin dynasty and the beginning of the Han dynasty. These works require careful study, for they show a perfected technique, a mature style and a developed symbolic language. The decorative calligraphy, like the meander motif in our

Vase with painted decoration
2500–2000 B.C.
Neolithic period. Yang-shao, Kansu
Earthware; height 7 2/3".

Yu bronze
1100–1000 B.C. End of Shang-ying period,
beginning of Chou period
Height 7 1/4″. This *yu* vase was used to
contain food.

illustration, is magnificent. In such bronzes we can sometimes observe a fearless tiger, the *t'ao t'ieh,* which translates, rather curiously, as "glutton." We can think of the animal as symbol of terror or as charm capable of exorcizing evil spirits. Eventually this fantastic creature loses his importance as a decorative feature and, on later bronzes, is represented only by a pair of staring eyes. This particular work excels for its exquisite form and noble beauty as well as for the rhythmic harmony between its shape and its calligraphic decorations.

Bronze chung
Fifth century B.C.
Period of the Fighting Kingdoms
Height 7 1/6″.

BRONZE CHUNG.   *Period of the Fighting Kingdoms.*
In 1927 B.C., the Chou sovereigns in Northern China (Shensi) routed the Shang-Yin dynasty and conquered their lands. They formed in the Yellow River valley a new dynasty under the central authority of a sovereign and various feudal lords who divided the kingdom into many small states. Each state gradually became stronger and stronger and eventually almost independent. The Shang, who were a much more noble and sophisticated people than the Chou, produced a very elegant art. Under the ascendancy of the Chou, their forms and decorations, like the *t'ao t'ieh,* little by little lost their importance and became mere ornament. This bronze *chung,* a bell decorated on both the outside and the inside, is a typical example from the

21

Low relief with dance and kitchen scenes
Second century A.D. Eastern Han or later
Detail. Limestone;
height 21 3/4", width 4 3/4", length 64 2/3".

late Chou period which is sometimes called the period of the Fighting King-doms (481–221 B.C.). Although it is difficult to make out, the decoration on its exterior seems to be a strangely shaped animal in union with a varied array of other beasts and birds. In the upper part we discern a pair of bird's talons and a large beak. On the left and right, two other birds are repre-sented with taloned claws and atop the lid is the face of an unidentified monster.

BRONZE LIEN. *Han Dynasty.*

This bronze is a circular receptacle with a lid (*lien*) and is dated in the Han dynasty (206 B.C.–200 A.D.). After a rare tomb painting at Ch'ang-sha (Hunan, fourth century B.C.), the first manifestations of art are to be found as paintings on terra-cotta tombstones, partially painted incisions on fu-nerary chamber stones, bronze mirrors and pottery and on sandstone pot-tery. Bronze *lien,* which were usually gilded or lacquered, were used as containers for such toilet articles as cosmetics and ceramic *lien* were used for funerary purposes. Their decorations usually consisted of low-relief heads of animals out of whose mouths hang rings and whose feet resemble bears' paws. Examples, like the one in the illustration, are rich in symbolic meaning. Svelte, arrogant animals are entwined in elegant plant-like spirals on the upper and lower bands. The supports are little bears who hold their noses between their forepaws. The lid of this work is the most important part, for the opulent decoration of the sacred mountain (*Po-sha*) which, in Taoist myth, is the heavenly paradise surrounded by the great ocean waves of the world.

22

Bronze Lien
Third century B.C.–third century A.D.
Han dynasty
Height 8 2/3", diameter 7 7/8".

LOW RELIEF WITH DANCE AND KITCHEN SCENES. *Eastern Han.* Many primitive civilizations decorated their tombs with worthy personages from government or nobility or celebrated warriors, but mostly with things that were dear to the deceased, such as people and animals he knew in life. In China the tombs were not adorned with gloomy death symbols nor religious allegories, but with lively scenes of historical events, mythical episodes, legends, hunts, feasts and daily life. Scenes of men on horseback are typical; they are usually small and airy depictions, showing the rider decked out in his fighting gear as a happy, aggressive, proud man. The scenes are complemented with birds, fish and trees whose branches weave into delightful patterns. Usually supernatural beings hover in the upper spaces or the realm of heaven. The technique is essentially flat without any feeling for three-dimensionality. The reliefs are carved or modeled directly on the stone. The background is rough and the figures smoothed out. Incisions cut into the figures emphatically outline their contours. Most of the important works have been found in the Szechwan and Shantung provinces. 23

It is difficult to single out their sources. We think of the hunt scene on Chou bronze vases (5000–3000 B.C.) or the bronze vases of the Fighting Kingdoms (480–221 B.C.) as possible prototypes. There are also references to Han terra-cotta tombstones, decorated lacquers and to the Fighting Kingdoms jades, and to the wall paintings in the palaces of the nobles. They even resemble the Liao-yang tombs of Manchuria. The most renowned and beautiful funerary chambers are those of the Wu family, built between 147 and 168 A.D. near Shantung. The stone slab in the illustration dates from the second century A.D. and depicts the family's daily activities. There is, for example, a kitchen with people cleaning fish and shooting birds. Neither noble nor heroic, the Wu chamber is homey and intimate and yet still typical of the poetic art that flourished during this period.

BUDDHA HEAD. *Northern Wei Dynasty.*

A fragment of a statuary group, this head of Buddha was found in the caves of a country temple in Yün-kang (Northern China). Such temples were carved into the hills in China in imitation of the temples along the caravan routes of Central Asia. Inside them, Buddhist sculptures were hewn from the living rock and occasionally paintings (*tun-huang*) were executed on the walls. The oldest temples date from the fourth and fifth centuries B.C. Like the ritual gestures (*mudrā*), the iconography of these sculptures has been defined according to Buddhist canon. Different stylistic accents, however, are found in different geographical regions. The historical origin of the Yün-kang temples goes back to 439 when To-pa nomads of Turkish origin conquered the Northern Lian dynasty (397–439), founded the Chinese Wei dynasty and established their first capital at Ta-t'ung (Shansi) and subsequently transferred it to Loyang (Honan). Zealots of the Buddist faith, they set about constructing the Yün-kang temples not far from Ta-t'ung. The first sculptures are reminiscent in style and iconography of the Indian and Central Asian Buddhas. In the sixth century the magnif-

Buddha head
Fourth century. Northern Wei dynasty
Stone; height 16 1/3".
Fragment from a Yün-kang temple.

24

icent works of Yün-kang were used as models for the lyrical cave figures of Lung-men (Honan) and later in the harmonious Sui dynasty temples (589–618). Following canonical writings, Buddha was to be represented with a stiff rigor in stance, clothing, coiffure and in his ritual gestures. Even though Buddha is a supernatural being with divine symbols, the contours of his body are made to come alive with a human vitality. His face is transfigured in a combination of thought and smile. Of the 32 major characteristics (*laksana*) which distinguish the superhuman perfection of Buddha, the *usnia,* a crowning protuberance of his head, is a symbol of Buddha's superhuman abilities and is a hallmark of his divinity. Everything about him is intellectual, of the mind, like thought frozen in stone. His hair and ears are hardly indicated. His face is but a glance which generates the light of thought and his smile is a glow of serenity, of life, which exists in an inner-found peace.

VASE WITH LID. *Sui Dynasty.*
This typical example of ancient Yueh ceramics, along with recently discovered similar objects, is dated to the sixth century A.D., during the Sui dynasty (589–618). Its ovoid shape is enlivened with incised decorations of lotus petals; handles with small holes are grouped in twos on the vase shoulder. A smooth and spotty brown glaze produces an effective surface.

RELIQUARY — CENTRAL–ASIA.
Among the objects brought to Japan from the Otani expedition that explored Central-Asia early in the twentieth century, this T'ang reliquary (618–906) was found in the ruins of Kucha, an old caravan center along the silk route. Its form is inspired from the symbolic *stupa,* the Buddhist monument of Indian origin designed to preserve Buddha's relics. It was turned in wood on a lathe, lined with a glued hemp, painted and covered with a transparent layer of lacquer. Its style is typically Central-Asiatic and employs the Chinese technique of applying lacquers to a pictorial decoration of Iranian taste. The colored decorations emphatically reveal a Sassanid influence in the motifs of *rotae* or wheel shapes and pearl-bordered medallions which were largely used by Persians in gold work and fabrics. Later, these elements were used in the applied arts of the Far East. The decoration consists of geometrical designs mingled with figurative scenes. On the cone-shaped lid, winged figures of music-making angels hover between medallions and winged fantasy creatures heraldically face each other.

WINGED HORSE. *Detail of pitcher decoration — T'ang Dynasty.* p. 28

The subject of the winged horse is rather exceptional in the figurative repertory of Far Eastern art. It appears at a breakneck gallop on this finely engraved gilded silver pitcher. The origin of the piece is obscure. We do not know precisely if it is Chinese or Japanese; but it is most likely Chinese, for the pitcher was probably taken to Japan and donated to Hisōji, one of the oldest Buddhist temples in the country. We learn this from an ancient inscription written in ink on the pitcher body. From Hisōji, the pitcher then passed into the collections of Horyuji of Nara. Its mouth and lid are shaped like the head of a dragon in a typical Chinese design of the mythical animal, which, in this case, is twisted into an exotic shape called by the Chinese a "pitcher of Western barbarians." Its name does not allude to its provenance but to a type of pottery that the Chinese goldsmith looked to for inspiration. It is a well-known fact that the Chinese, like the ancient Greeks, designated barbarian all peoples whom they had not absorbed into their civilization or who lived out of range of their influence. "Western barbarians" were gener-

CENTRAL–ASIA
Reliquary
Seventh century A.D.
Lacquered cloth on wood;
height 12 1/2", diameter 13".

Vase with lid
Sixth century A.D. Sui dynasty
Glazed earthware; height 9 1/2", diameter of the mouth 4 1/3", diameter of the base 4".

Winged horse
Detail of pitcher decoration
Seventh century A.D. T'ang dynasty
Gilt silver; height 19 2/3". From Horyuji,
this work is classified among the
national treasures of Japan.

ically all peoples who lived west of China, but later the name came to apply specifically to the peoples of Iran with whom the Chinese had established commercial contacts during the Christian era. The "animalistic" decoration and the form of this pitcher show Persian-Sassanid influences.

AMPHORA. *T'ang Dynasty.*

A strong sculptural form marks the structure of this amphora, the mouth of which is being bitten by two long-necked dragons. It is a descendant of Iranian and perhaps other western Asian prototypes and its medallion-covered ornamentation was certainly inspired by such western works as the Syrian glass amphorae which Chinese potters sometimes used as sources for striated designs and crested handles. This type of vase was popular in T'ang China (618–906) and a certain number of them has been found among tomb objects of the period. They are mostly made of porcelain; a few are made of glazed terra cotta. In the illustrated example, we see a typical three-color glaze (*san ts'ai*) and a decoration which consists of an "egg and spinach" design highlighted by an uneven flow of colors. Such a technique gives accentuated relief to the stylized flower in the central medallion.

Amphora
Eighth century A.D. T'ang dynasty
Glazed earthware; height 18 3/4";
diameter of the mouth 4 1/2",
diameter of the base 4".
Classified among the most
important national treasures.

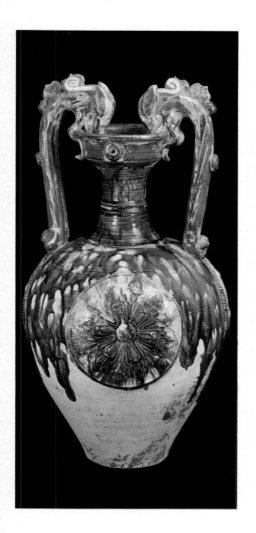

BRONZE MIRROR. *Nara Period.* p. 30

From the beginning of the Bronze Age, mirrors played a major role in Japanese metal-work. Endowed with special magic and symbolic properties, mirrors conjured up ideas of the powers of the sun and of imperial rule. They were generally made of bronze and were molded into a disc-like form with raised edges and a smooth reflecting surface. They had no handles, but were provided on the back with a rounded projection, similar to a button which has been perforated and through which a cord can be slipped. The face of the mirror was decorated with designs in relief. Identical to Chinese mirrors, Japanese mirrors were undoubtedly inspired by Chinese or Korean models. Early local efforts were usually inferior in both technique and refinement of design. Later, indigenous designs noticeably improved, but continued to echo the same themes as the Chinese prototypes. Sometimes, however, the imitation worked, as in the case of certain mirrors which reproduce in an attentive linear fashion the same simple geometric compositions of the Chinese original. Since the Japanese did not understand the iconographical significance of Taoist symbols, their designs had only a formal meaning and often were copied with little agility.

The illustrated example is exceptional. Presumably cast in the lost-wax technique, it presents an extraordinarily fine composition. The design is dominated by an interesting stylization of landscape elements, particularly of spiraling sea waves. Symmetrically grouped, four islands loom up from the sea. Vegetation, birds and a few animals enliven the hills and there is a figure seated upon a bank. Perspective has not been a concern of the artist. In the water we see fish and birds and two people, one of whom is depicted in a boat. The subject is Taoist and represents the Islands of the Blessed, which, if discovered, yield the elixir of immortality. Thus the mirror becomes a prophetic symbol or charm for the person to whom it was dedicated. According to the notes of the Horyuji of Nara, we only know that the mirror was offered to the Buddhist temple of the Empress Komei in 736 upon the anniversary of Prince Shotoku's death. The period in which it was made is not known nor is it known whether the work is Chinese or Japanese. The spiral treatment of the waves as well as the miniature annotations concerning the symbolic significance and the singular stylist perfection of the islands would make us think that the work is from a Chinese hand.

CENTRAL–ASIA
Figures under a Tree
Eighth century
Painting on paper; 56″ by 22″.
Found at Turfan.
Classified among the important
national treasures.

FIGURES UNDER A TREE. *Central–Asia.*

Because of its geographical diversities, racial mixtures and blending of cultures, Central Asia produced a multiform art which indiscriminately criss-

CHINESE OR JAPANESE BRONZE
Mirror
Eighth century A.D. Nara period
Diameter 18 1/2″. From Horyuji;
classified among national treasures.

crossed old and new formal and symbolic characteristics. A unique case in history and ethnography, like a vast melting pot included the nomadic peoples of the Greco-Hellenistic and western Roman civilizations and the cultures of Iran, Tibet, India and China. This area, moreover, since the most ancient times, created a geographical tie between the West and the Orient through the two principal caravan routes to the north and south from Bamiyan in Afghanistan to Tunhuang near the Kansu border. Tunhuang, indeed, became a cultural and artistic center because of its strong municipal government and disciplined Chinese army. Under its protection, major centers such as Qyzil, Kucha, Miran, Turfa, Khotan, Bazaklik and Dandan-Uiliq were able to flourish. The painting reproduced here belongs to the T'ang Dynasty and comes from a tomb of eastern Kara-khoja, near Turfan. The figure and his servant do not have Chinese features. They are represented taking off a mantle that falls amply onto the shoulders and chest. A roll of paper at the belt indicates an intellectual or a noble, called a *wen-jen,* who is a man who surpasses others with his profound knowledge. Figures placed under trees are a common iconographical subject in Central-Asian art. In this case, there is also a woman, perhaps the man's wife, under the tree. Almost impossible to define according to the Chinese esthetic, these paintings smack of a special pictorial language, barbaric and foreign to the severe classicism of the cosmopolitan T'ang Dynasty.

THE BODHISATTVA KSITIGARBHA. *T'ang Dynasty.*
The form of Buddhism called *Mahayana* (the Great Vehicle), which is later than the *Hinayana* (the Little Vehicle), is a meditative, transcendental and charitable mysticism. More human in essence than most primitive asceticisms, it created its own pantheon of Bodhisattvas. A Bodhisattva is a being, in keeping with the first meaning of the Sanskrit word, whose essence (*sattva*) is enlightenment (*bodhi*). Arriving almost at the limit of the supreme perfection of Buddha, the Bodhisattva renounces Buddha in a supreme sacrifice in order to stay among men, working on their salvation at the risk of losing his own. The early visual art that such myths prompted is anonymous and its iconography does not always conform to canonical texts and Confucian creeds. Rather, it relates to popular ideas and to a Taoist mysticism. The figure in our illustration is a Bodhisattva which, in its Chinese incarnation, carries the name Ti-tsang. He is merciful and usually carries in one hand a staff with six rings whose touch can open the doors of

Bodhisattva Ksitiar
Eighth-ninth century. T'ang dynasty
This is a painting on a sacred banner of
thin silk, found by
Paul Pelliot in 1908 on one of
his expeditions to Tun-huang.
33 2/5″ × 7″.

33

Ade and he carries in the other hand a flamboyant pearl that illuminates the shadowy land of the condemned. Here, however, he is represented without these attributes.

His hands are depicted in vague ritual gestures with the iconographical liberty that artists took with such images. Artists depended more often on traditions and popular legends than on strict iconography. Although the colors are boldly contrasted, they discreetly enhance the linear outlining of the figure and his clothes. The decoration above the head, shaped like a canopy, is a common Buddist motif in the T'ang style. This example is important, if anonymous, since we have no other historically authenticated works from the master T'ang painters.

SHIH-K'O *Two Patriarchs Purifying Their Hear* Middle of the tenth century. Period of the Five dynasties. Two kakemono painted with ink on paper; 14 1/5″ × 25 1/2″ each. Classified among the important national treasures.

SHIH–K'O. *Two Patriarchs Purifying Their Hearts.*
Kakemono is the name most commonly used in the West to indicate Far Eastern paintings executed on a strip of silk paper. Kakemono were usually

rolled on a pole to which they were attached and which served to hang them on a wall. The word is Japanese and means "object for hanging." *Makimono* means "object for rolling" and refers to paintings which unroll from right to left in harmony with the sequence of a story. In the West, these words are also used for Chinese paintings for which the proper names would be *Chuan,* "scroll" (for hanging), and *chüan wu* (more generically "rolling object").

The illustrated work is one of the best examples of ink painting in the stained style which is called *p'o-mo* (ink stain) in Chinese. The name refers to the origin of landscape painting by Wang Wei (699–759). This medium was preferred by the painter-poets of the glorious Sung period (960–1279) and because of its figurative conciseness, was adopted by the Ch'an sect disciples. Their religion is better known in the West by its Japanese name Zen. Ascetic, without doctrine, strictly individual and essential, this sect simplified methods of figurative expression and gave full rein to its basic artistic intuition. In its evocative power, elegance, incision, *Ch'an* painting is related to ideographic writing and is a superb example of the ability to transform immediately a mental process into a visual image.

35

Vase with bird head
Eleventh century. Liao dynasty
Glazed earthware; height 15 1/5",
diameter of the mouth 4",
diameter of the base 3".

VASE WITH BIRD HEAD. *Liao Dynasty.*

With a mouth in the shape of a bird's head, this vase imitates the T'ang phoenix pitchers. This bird's head seems more alive, however, with the élan and harmonious structure in its long molded neck. The lines of the neck are repeated in the foot of the vase, which is closer in spirit to T'ang ceramics than to similar works by the nomads who started such "animal-istic" decorations. The vase is a product of the Liao factories which took their name from the Central-Asian dynasty that dominated Northern China from 907 to 1125. The period brought about a fusion of Chinese and Central-Asian traditions in the plastic arts. The pottery centers of Ting-chou and Tz'u-chou favored a revival of decorative T'ang techniques in a monochromatic glaze, the use of the "three-colors" techniques and specific ornamental elements. The illustrated piece, however, also betrays an influence from the Sung period, manifested in the black-outlined flower and leaf designs and the thick green glaze.

PITCHER. *Northern Sung Dynasty.*

This heavily repaired example was found in a Korean tomb; it is, neverthe-less, a Chinese work and belongs to the Yao pottery type with intaglio dec-

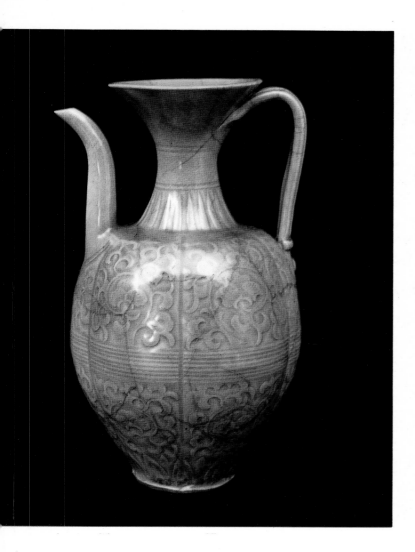

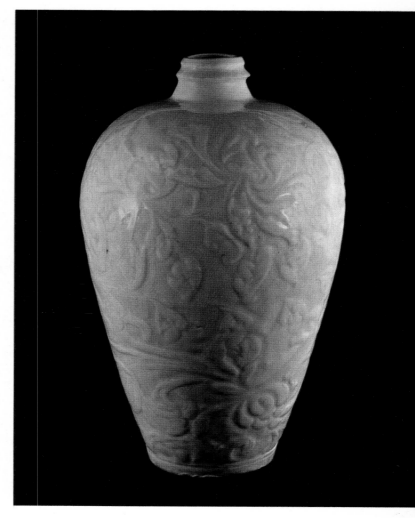

Pitcher
Eleventh century. Northern Sung dynasty
Celadon; height 11 1/2",
diameter of the mouth, 4 1/5",
diameter of the base 2 4/5".

oration. The leaves-and-peonies motif is distributed in horizontal zones and the glazing is very thin. The piece probably comes from the northwest Shensi kilns, known as the Yao-Chou, which made an olive-green glazed pottery, usually called the "celadon of the north." In China they were called *chun* and were highly prized because of their brilliant opalescence. A mixture of ricestraw in the pigments gives such pitchers the extraordinary quality of transmitting a beautiful shimmering effect.

Vase
Eleventh-twelfth century. Southern Sung dynasty. Glazed earthware; height 15", diameter of the mouth 2", diameter of the base 4 3/5". This example was found in 1916 in Japan near Ibaraki, along with a stupa-form reliquary of the Kamakura period (1185–1333).

VASE. *Southern Sung Dynasty.*

Peonies in low relief on a striped background decorate this vase, called because of its shape *mei-p'ing,* which means it was designed to hold a plum branch. It was also used to hold rice wine. Widely appreciated in both China and Korea, the bottle-like vessel has shoulders which gradually taper to the base. Such vases were important in Japan and in the southern areas of China where numerous factories, especially along the coastal zone of Kiangsi and Kuangtun, were located. It seems that the first vases were produced for a very refined clientele by potters near Ching-te-chen in Kiangsi. The potters applied pale blue glazings to terra cottas and porcelains and they were called *ch'ing-pai* (bluish white) or *ying-ch'ing* (hazy blue). They are famous for their suffused powdery tonalities.

KUAN TYPE CHIAO–TAN CUP OF BLUE PORCELAIN (ALTAR OF HEAVEN). *Southern Sung Dynasty.*

Even though the Chinese considered only painting and calligraphy as visual arts, nevertheless sculpture and ceramics were highly developed. Ceramics of the Sung period, for example, achieved near-perfection in technique and beauty of color and material. They were manufactured in imperial workshops for court use or for official ceremonies and their name, *Kuan-yao,* means "state kilns." The glazed cup in the illustration belongs to the noble celadon family. Such earthware usually was named after its color. But "celadon" comes from the hero of a seventeenth-century French romance, *Astrée,* by Honoré d'Urfé and refers to a pale, languishing green mixed with white. The shape of this slender cup is like two hands which have joined to form a hollow and then separate in a slow rise. Added more for protection than for enrichment, a metallic border undulates with subtle floral decorations. The color is undefinable. It is like musical variations of rising and falling pale green. Light seems to shine through the color, as through translucent skin.

VASE WITH PLUM BRANCHES. *Korea.*

Like the Chinese *mei-p'ing* vases, this Korean example vibrates with stylized elegance. Its classical river landscape, alive with water birds, insects, bam-

Chiao-tan blue porcelain cup of the Kuan type (Altar of Heaven)
Twelfth century. Southern Sung dynasty
Porcelain; height 3 1/2",
diameter of the mouth 10 1/2",
diameter of the base 2 4/5".
Classified among the important
national treasures.

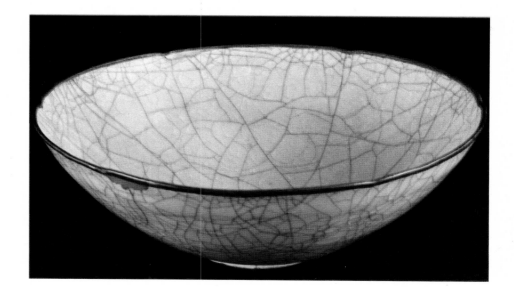

KOREA
Vase with Plum Branches
Twelfth-thirteenth century
Celadon; height 13 1/2",
diameter of the mouth 2 1/5",
diameter of the base 5 1/5".

boo trees and plum branches, achieves a pictorial lyricism through its mastery of atmospheric sensitivity. An antecedent of celadon glazing technique which the Koreans assimilated and mastered, the grayish-green enamel of this vase leaves something to be desired.

LI LUNG-MIEN(?)
Circa 1040–1106
Imaginary Voyage into the Hsiao-hsiang Region
Second half of the twelfth century. Southern Sung dynasty. Scroll painted with ink on paper 12″ × 161″. Classified national treasure.

LI LUNG–MIEN(?). *Imaginary Voyage into the Hsiao-hsiang Region.*
The subject of this painting refers to a twelfth-century text: after traveling for 30 years to the most famous places where intellectuals gathered, Yuan-chao, a monk of the *Ch'an* sect, became embittered for not having been able to visit the Hsiao-hsiang region by the Tung-ting lake. Every time he met a famous painter, he would ask for a painting of the place. The scroll reproduced here represents that region with the historical Yang-tse-kiang River meandering through the surrounding hills. The scroll is signed Po-shih, a *tzu* or artistic pseudonym of the famous Li Kung-lin. He was better known by the name of Li Lung-mien (circa 1040–1106) after the place where he lived and died. He was celebrated, above all, as a painter of the magnificent horses which were presented to the emperor as signs of homage and obedience. He was also known for his Buddhist figures and sumptuous landscapes, such as this one, with towering mountains, clear, calm valleys, mirror-like lakes and delicate coppices. He was so famous that forgeries of his works were made while he was still alive. Thus the landscape in the illustration possibly might be a copy.

LIANG K'AI. *Landscape with Snow.* p. 42
Snow scenes were much cherished in Chinese painting after Wang Wei (699–759) did his famous *Clearing after the Snowstorm* and *Snowy Mountain Landscape*. In the Ming and Ch'ing dynasties, snow in itself, as a realistic phenomenon, interested artists, whereas before, snow simply served to turn the landscape into a fantastic scene. In this painting by Liang K'ai, two cloaked men on their tired mounts are dwarfed by infinite space and dizzying mountains. In one corner of the painting tree branches are

40

董跋謂顧氏名
卷有四今乃散
而後合示異豐
城之遇也乾隆
御識

LIANG K'AI
Active circa 1200
Landscape with Snow
Beginning of the thirteenth century.
Southern Sung dynasty
Kakemono painted with
ink and washes on canvas; 44″ × 20″.
National treasure.

reduced to splinters, indicating to us what a rough winter it has been and also as a symbol of death. Yet as one of the men turns to talk to the other he creates a moment of life amid the oppressive desolation.

LIAN K'AI. *Portrait of the Poet Li Po.*   *p. 44*

For the spiritual biography of Lian K'ai (active around 1200) it is sufficient to remember that he, after having enjoyed the highest academic recognition for his art as the *tai-chao* (painter in service: the eminent official title given to painters of the Court) and won the Order of the Golden Belt, he renounced worldly glories and withdrew to Liu-t'ung in a monastery of *Ch'an* Buddhism as a humble novice. It is necessary to explain briefly what this sect meant and the significance of the *Ch'an* doctrine. Coming from the Sanskrit *Dhyana,* Zen in Japanese, it can be approximately translated as "meditation." In spirit and practice this doctrine is the individual discipline of thought through which conventional language limitations are transcended. With intuition, it is possible to arrive at the supreme level of enlightenment (*satori*) that leads to a state of grace, to an absolute mental knowledge of the world and its being.

We can thus understand why this sect preferred the simplest means, using only ink (*Ch'an p'o hua*) in their art, and a simple technique (*p'o-mo*) of blots and stains, without any niceties of shading or modeling.

The brush stroke is rapid, very fluid. Thought is reduced to a notation, a mere symbolic sign of a mental image. Even historical, legendary and religious figures are conceived as simply as possible. In the spirit of subject and technique in ink painting, Liang-K'ai was one of the great artists of his time and of all time — because of his nobility of thought and the perfection of his expressive means. Two of his principal works, *Penitent Sakyamuni* and *Winter Landscape* (which is attributed to him), are executed in a light-and-dark ink technique which achieve coloristic effects. Others, like the *Patriarch Hui-nêng* and the *Portrait of the Poet Li Po* are almost musical evocations of a mental image in the manner of the *Ch'an* technique. Li Po

43

LIANG K'AI
Portrait of the Poet Li Po
Beginning of the thirteenth century.
Southern Sung dynasty
Kakemono painted with ink on paper;
31 2/3″ × 12″. Classified among
national treasures.

was among the greatest poets of the T'ang Dynasty (618–906) and his verse is a lyrical incantation of clouds, heaven, moon, mountains, seasons, beautiful women, flowers and drunkenness. Certainly Liang K'ai remembered this. He pictured the poet as he walked ecstatically in the valleys, only his face and his feet showing from the cloak that fully conceals him.

LIANG K'AI. *The Sixth Patriarch Cutting a Bamboo.*   p. 45

By the same master of *Portrait of Li Po*, this painting is more emphatic in the use of the *Ch'an* technique. Hui-nêng, the figure who is represented, is the sixth patriarch of the Zen Buddhist sect. He was known for his high-flying thoughts but Liang K'ai preferred to paint him cutting off the leaves of a bamboo shoot. Manual labor was recommended by the *Ch'an* sect. The artist has used a minimum of means to achieve a maximum of effect. Hui-nêng is summarily defined and it looks as if his knife was executed in one swoop of the brush. The tree behind is a mere stroke which vanishes at the side of the painting. The rest is dramatic open space.

MA YUAN. *Solitary Fisherman on the River.*   pp. 46–47

In the late period of the Southern Sung (1127–1279), after the Mongol invasion, the capital was transferred from K'ai-feng in the North to Hang-chou in the South. With purer techniques art started to transpose poetry

LIANG K'AI
The Sixth Patriach Cutting a Bamboo
Beginning of the thirteenth century.
Southern Sung dynasty
This painting recalls another equally
famous work: *Hui-neng Furiously Ripping
up a Sutra* (a Buddhist writing) which is in
the Tokyo National Museum.
Kakemono painted with ink on paper;
29″ × 12 1/2″.
Classified among important
national treasures.

into visual terms. Landscape painting in particular, much like its philosophical and literary counterparts, went beyond its previous possibilities. Ma Yuan was one of the great masters of this time. A painter of landscapes, figures, flowers and birds, he was active between 1190 and 1224. The paint-

MA YUAN
Active between 1190 and 1224
Solitary Fisherman on the River
First half of the thirteenth century.
Southern Sung dynasty
Kakemono painted with ink on silk;
10 5/8″ × 19 3/4″.
National treasure.

ing reproduced in the illustration is attributed to him for good reason. In some of his works, Yuan, as well as Hsia Kuei (active around 1130–1230), expresses a type of lyrical painting in which landscape and abstract dreamy thought are one. It is as if creative ecstasy and the worldless image were to meet in an infinite space of light. This is the proper classic Sung spirit: pureness of line, profundity of philosophical thought, high-pitched melancholy, dignity of theme. The drama of the scene is keyed to one figure, like the fisherman in a boat, gazing at his line. Only the fisherman and his story are figurative; the water and sky haze into vagueness. Only a few lines near the boat reveal the presence of the water and the vast spaces around the boat suggest solitude and infinity.

FENG TZU–CHEN. *Calligraphy.* *p. 48*

For most Westerners, calligraphy means nothing more than, literally, beautiful writing. It is used on diplomas, greeting cards, anniversary and wedding invitations. But for Orientals, calligraphy is an art like painting, appreciated as both a pictorial and ideographic representation. The Chinese esthetic, in fact, curiously excludes sculpture from its list of the fine arts, considering it a manual labor, but emphasizes calligraphy.

The fusion of an idea and an image, calligraphy carries with it not only connotations of legible signs but also a design. Calligraphy derived from the type of writing which was defined in the late Han period (25–220 A.D.) and underwent changes in various regions and times. It went from the simple stylistic invention of the Shang-Ying dynasty (1700–1028 B.C.) to the elegant flourishes of the Yuan dynasty (1280–1368). Some of the types are the *k'ai shu* or the "regular writing" style, the *hsing shu* or the "fluid writing" style and the *ts'ao shu* or the "grass writing" style. Our illustration is an example of the last type and was done by Feng Tzu-chen, who lived in the first half of the fourteenth century. He was famous as an intellectual and calligrapher. The "grass writing" style was inspired by Huang Ting-chien, of the four great calligraphers of the Sung period (960–1279 A.D.),

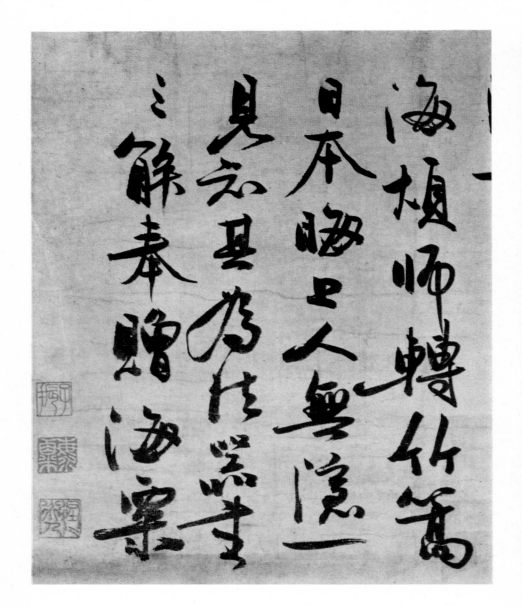

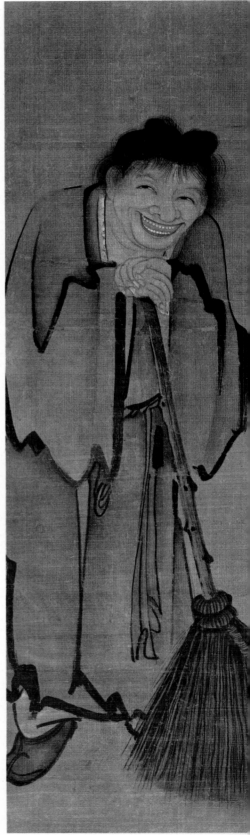

FENG TZU-CHEN
Calligraphy
First half of the fourteenth century.
Yuan dynasty
Kakemono ink calligraphy on paper;
13″ × 40″.
48 Classified among national treasures.

and in feeling was free, varied and mobile, like meadow grass. The interesting rhythms Tzu-chen created between the solids of the ink and the voids of the white background are really an art of black and white, a rhythm of space and shape.

YEN HUI
Hain-Shan and Shih-te
Fourteenth century. Yuan dynasty
Two silk kakemonos representing
Taoist genii;
51″ × 16 1/8″.
Classified among national treasures.

YEN HUI. *Han-shan and Shih-te (Taoist Genii).*

Although Yen Hui was traditional in his subject matter, he was an innovator in his spirit and form. We do not know his dates, but only that he worked in the fourteenth century and that he adopted the name of Yuang (1280–1368). He preferred to paint religious figures such as monks, ascetics and Taoist genii and his circumstantial representations of them suggest portraits. Unlike the distorted religious figures of Huan Hsiu (832–912), Yen Hui's figures pay no attention to iconographical traditions and become individual studies of personalities. The Taoist genii Han-shan and Shih-te are always figured together. Created by Oriental mythography, Han-shan symbolizes theory and Shih-te symbolizes practice, a ideal combination of the ideological and the empirical. Han-shan is usually shown with a white scroll, indicating the pureness of his thought and Shih-te, with a broom, indicating his contact with the world. Both figures have similar faces and smiles and floppy clothing. Little can be said about Yen Hui due to the scarceness of his extant works. None of his paintings is signed and therefore they are only attributed to him. His landscapes do not rise above the mediocre, but his religious figures are unequalled.

LANDSCAPES. *Yuan Dynasty.*

Placed side by side, these two paintings form an inseparable whole. In their lyricism they recall the classic Sung artists and in their inventiveness they make us think of the Yuan artists who did not allow their painting to be sapped by academic rules. The paintings indulge in sensual and full-blown forms for the delightful sake of forms themselves. The works were originally attributed to Kai Jan-hui, a fifteenth-century painter whom some identify with Kao K'o-kung (1248–1310). Others think they are replicas of works by Kao K'o-ming, who was active around 1020. Even if we cannot be sure of the author of these works, we are sure that we are in the presence of a grand and creative sensibility.

Landscapes
Second half of the fourteenth century. End of Yuan, beginning of Ming dynasty. Two kakemonos, ink on paper; 21 1/3″ × 9 1/4″ each; to judge from the style, they can be dated to the end of the Yuan dynasty (1280–1368) and the beginning of the Ming dynasty (1368–1614). Classified among the national treasures.

BLUE–AND–WHITE VASE. *Yuan Dynasty.*   *p. 52*

Sandstone porcelain was first used as a material in China in the Han period (206 B.C.–221 A.D.). It was a particular favorite of the Six Dynasties period (221–586) and of the T'ang dynasty (618–906). From these periods, we have a profusion of excellent examples of sandstone porcelain craftsmanship of all types, from the beautiful whites to the resplendent "three-color" glazes (*san-ts'ai*). It was the Sung dynasty, however, which perfected the form, color and style of sandstone porcelain, turning this type of earthware into a noble art. The Yuan dynasty continued to make vases out of this material, but without the flair and inspiration of the Sung potters. Unlike the simple Sung decorations, Yuan wares were bedecked with complicated floral designs in multi-colored glazes. Yuan potters imported from Persia and other countries in Central Asia new techniques which produced works like the blue ceramics from the Ying-te-chen kilns. The vase in our illustration does not have the airy lightness of the Sung porcelains, but it is solid, well defined and its functional purpose is highly evident. The decoration of the fish which wriggles through algae-filled water is lively and vibrant and the subtle blues of the glaze make this work a rare beauty.

BLUE–AND–WHITE DISH.   *Ming Dynasty*.
The manufacture of "blue-and-white" porcelain started in China toward the end of the Yuan dynasty (1260–1368) with the availability of pure

Blue-and-white vase with fish and algae
Fourteenth century. Yuan dynasty
Porcelain; height, 10 7/8",
diameter of mouth 6 3/4",
diameter of base 6 5/8".
National treasure.

cobalt mineral imported from Persia. This "Mohammedan blue," as it is sometimes called, was also the result of a new and perfected technique. The best porcelains date from the beginning of the Ming dynasty (1368–1644). The example here is undoubtedly one of the most beautiful. The central circle displays a luxuriant lotus plant with flowers and buds: a symbol of purity and prosperity repeated in a continuous floral frieze in the middle band. In contrast with the fluidity of the central composition, the outer edge heavily frames the piece with rigid wave-like acanthus leaves.

Blue-and-white dish with floral decoration
First half of the fifteenth century.
Ming dynasty
Porcelain; height, 3 1/2″; diameter 17 1/2″.
National treasure.

LI TSAI. *Landscape.*

Li Tsai, a court painter during the reign of Hsuan-te (1426–1435), is considered among the greatest artists of his time. He followed the traditions of the great masters of the past, above all those of the Chê School. In his compositions he did not follow the dictates of his fantasy but composed within the stringent limits of past examples. Thus he echoed in some details Kuo Hsi (circa 1020–1090) and in others the inseparable duo of Ma Yuan (active circa 1190–1224) and Hsia Kuei (active circa 1180–1230). This landscape makes evident how it was conceived in its essence from an ideal vision and intellectually constructed with elements from other, older works. The mountains rise boldly toward the sky, towering over a small temple in their midst. Small figures are overwhelmed by the immense panorama, perhaps symbolizing man's dependence on the great natural forces. Even without the dreamy lyricism of the Sung landscapes, this painting swells with dignity in its technical mastery and robust, realistic accents.

LI TSAI
Landscape
Middle fifteenth century. Ming dynasty
Kakemono, ink and colored washes on silk;
55 7/8″ × 33 1/2″.
Classified among national treasures.

LU–CHI. *Birds and Flowers of the Four Seasons.* pp. 56–57

Lu-Chi's fame is usually connected with paintings of birds and flowers which were executed about 1477–1505 during the Ming dynasty. Like the *wên jên hua* paintings of the intellectual school, these works are technically perfect and preciously decorative. The composition reproduced here is evidently an allegory of spring. The romantic languor of the small birds is offset by the bursting vigor of the winding, nervous branches. The slender and subtle twig is a symbol of the world's eternal spring. With its soft breath of peonies, sinuous trees and lively singing birds, the painting becomes a musical allegory of the sweetest season of the year.

On pages 56–57:
LU-CHI
Active between 1477 and 1505
Birds and Flowers of the Four Seasons
Beginning of sixteenth century.
Ming dynasty
Four kakemonos painted on silk;
69 1/2″ × 40 3/8″.
Classified among national treasures. Detail.

54

CHU–TUAN. *Landscape with Snow.*

A court painter for Emperor Wu-tsung (1506–1521) in the Cheng-teh period, Chu-tuan was born in the Ming dynasty (1368–1644) which followed the Yuan Mongolian conquest. After almost a century of foreign domination, the arts had evolved toward a pictorial sensualism and the enjoyment of forms and shapes for themselves. Emptied of symbolism and spiritual significance, the works became narrative or descriptive in feeling. Then the return to pure lyricism of the "gentlemen painters" school began which, centuries later, was replaced by conceptual "intellectual painting" (*wên jên hua*). The eventual return to a new academicism fostered a close study of the traditions of the great historic periods in art and politics. Servile imitation was avoided by the enlivened conscience of reacquired national dignity and the observance of the Confucian, Taoist and Buddhist religions, potent ideas from the past that turned into major forces in this renaissance. It may be said that Chu-tuan is responsible for a renewed interest in fantasy. But he worshipped the past. He looked to Ma Yuan (1190–1224) for landscapes; Lu Chu (active about 1470–1500) for birds and flowers; Wang Chi and Sheng Mon (fourteenth century) for human figures and to Hsia Ch'ang (1388–1470) for bamboo. The lyrical and fantastic Ma Yuan was his main teacher, but this does not show in the work illustrated here, which was inspired by the Chê school of the Southern Sung style. A characteristic of Chu-tuan is the incisive description of details that are emphasized without disturbing stylistic unity. This can be observed in the wintry landscape where trees grow from snow-covered rocks and distant mountains gradually shade off into the horizon. The small fisherman intently watching his pole from a shabby boat is a minor episode in a great white symphony. Man, who might be master of certain spiritual forces, is, in turn, dominated by the icy forces of nature.

CHU-TUAN
Landscape with Snow
First half of the sixteenth century.
Ming dynasty
Kakemono, ink and washes of color on silk;
68 3/4″ × 43 1/2″.
Classified as a national treasure.

QUADRANGULAR VASE. *Ming Dynasty.*   *p. 61*

This vase with a square mouth was made in two parts which were united with a technique reminiscent of the one used for bronze and other metal pottery. An example of "five colors" (*wu-ts'ai*) decoration, it combines cobalt blue with other metallic colors, covering them with a pure white enamel which has been slightly tinted with blue. A seal on the bottom dates the piece to the kingdom of Emperor Lung-ching (1567–1572). We can classify this work among the first examples of the style in vogue in the Wan-li period (1579–1620), called the style of "contrasting colors," in which the lively tones of enamel contrast with blue border lines. It is a kind of porcelain that was favored by European markets, so much, in fact, that massive export demands stimulated serial production of inferior quality. The example illustrated, however, is a precious piece. The decoration is distributed in three zones on the vase: dragon figures above, vegetable motifs below and in the center, and a landscape with birds, trees and flowers inside the blue-bordered medallions.

Quadrangular vase
Second half of the sixteenth century. Ming dynasty. Porcelain; height, 8 1/2″, width of mouth, 3 2/3″, width of base 3 3/4″. Reproduced actual size.

TIEN SHÊNG. *Bamboo.*   *p. 62*

Painting of bamboo was particularly favored during the Sung (960–1279) and the Yuan landscapist periods (1280–1368) by the intellectual school of "the poet's painting." This is easy to understand if we remember that Chinese painting derives from writing and calligraphy, graphic representations of thoughts and things. It is often said that flexible and robust bamboo symbolizes the man who falls and rises under the blows of adversity. But we should recall, perhaps, how much these vegetable forms with their slender, elegant small-leaved branches which constantly tremble with life lend themselves to the rapid brush strokes of calligraphy. That is why the subject was beloved by painters, poets, and calligraphers. Among the greatest of artists who painted bamboo are Kuo-Hsi (1020–1090); Sushih, better known by the name of Su T'ung-po (circa 1036–1101); Wên T'ung (1049–1079) and Mi Fei (1051–1107).

Tien Shêng lived at the beginning of the last Ch'ing dynasty (1644–1912), right after the renaissance of the preceding Ming dynasty. He looked back to the past for inspiration in this "bamboo" painting on a screen. The shadows almost become color in the brush strokes of the branches done in the *fei-po* technique (which lets "flying white" spaces sporadically appear through the ink). The calligraphic nature of this painting, clearly expressed by the ink and the shape of the individual strokes, is accentuated by the verses written in a highly idiosyncratic character and style. This was done not only figuratively, as is possible with ideograms, but also in the literary spirit of the composition. In the verses Shêng remembers bamboo leaves turning with the sun or the moon, their shadows on a wall or on a sheet of paper as he rested under them in contemplation.

On page 62:
TIEN SHENG
1693–1765
Bamboo (1735)
Ch'ing dynasty
Four-panel screen; ink on paper
47 7/8″ × 94″.

余家有茅屋數間南面種竹夏
日新篁初放綠陰照人置一小
榻其中甚涼適也秋冬之際取圍
屏骨子斷去兩頭橫安以為窗
櫺用勻薄潔白之紙糊之風和
日暖凍蠅觸窗紙上冬冬
作小鼓聲於時一片竹影
零亂豈非天然圖畫
乎凡吾畫竹無所師承
多得於紙窗粉壁
日光月影中耳

JAPAN

VASE. *Middle Jomon Period.*

This is a typical example of ceramic art from archaic Japan (Middle Jomon period, III–II millennium). Its elementary functional shape is enriched with decorations on the bare surfaces in order to satisfy the esthetic needs of a developing civilization. The useful object, in other words, also becomes a pleasure to the eyes; hence, the application of "rope" on still-fresh clay. The name Jomon means "rope decorations." Done casually and probably not according to a preconceived scheme, the decorations become more soberly spaced as the style developed, line and circles more rigorously modulated, until they reach their peak in the late figurative designs. The Jomon period never produced painted earthenware; the only color added was simply a basic red, a reference to blood. The example illustrated is one of the most beautiful of its kind. The rope motif follows the gesture of the hand that coiled it in linear, almost calligraphic rhythms and comes together in what could be an optical illusion or an intentional gesture as an isolated, vaguely human figure (with a spiral for a head, slender trunk and multiple arms) inserts itself into the meanders of the scheme.

CLAY FIGURINE. *Middle Jomon Period.* p. 66

We do not find the human figure in archaic Japanese sculpture and it is difficult to interpret the first representation of human beings, like this one from the Middle Jomon period (third-second century B.C.). They are called *"dogu"* in Japanese, or clay statuettes, and we find similar figures on pottery. Because of its head, both beastlike and human, the figure might have been used for magical practices perhaps as a charm to ward off evil. Its face is uglified by huge strong jaws, oblique, catlike eyes, and a grotesque hare-lip which distorts the entire lower portion. The little monster brings his

64

Vase
3000–2000 B.C. Middle Jomon period
Terra cotta; height, 23 2/3",
diameter of mouth 13 1/4".
Found at Miyanomae, district of Nagano.

Clay figurine
3000–2000 B.C. Middle Jomon period
Terra cotta; height, 10″,
shoulder width 8 3/8″.
Found at Kamikurogoma. Misaka-cho,
district of Yamamashi.

three-fingered hand back to his chest in what might be a symbolic or ritual gesture. The shoulders and parts of the figure's chest are covered with small scale-like holes. All told, this creature seems to have been created for a supernatural power by an intelligence that was half-human, half-animal.

ANTHROPOMORPHIC VASE. *Middle Yayoi Period.*

During the period when the Jomon were primarily a hunting and fishing culture the human figure played a major role in sculpture. These people

Anthropomorphic vase
First-second century A.D.
Middle Yayoi period
Terra cotta; height, 27 9/16″,
maximum diameter 11 7/16″.
From Osagata, Shimodate, district of Ibaraki.
Detail.

67

probably used these clay figures (*dogu*) as talismans in their adventurous and risky lives or as fetishes in magic or religious rituals. After millennia, Jomon was absorbed into the Yayoi culture which is named for the place where its handmade objects were first found. It was a more sedentary, evolved, and predominantly agricultural culture. The *dogu* almost disappeared and the human figure was relegated as a top to large vases, used for keeping cereals. The receptacle in the illustration was probably placed in the ground with only the head sticking out and either solid or liquid materials were poured into it. Most of the vase is smooth. The geometric designs which decorated the earlier Jomon works have disappeared. Also unlike the Jomon figures, the Yayoi works turn to total distortion of human characteristics. Because of his solemnity, fanlike beard, intent eyes and authoritative expression this figure could possibly be an ancient patriarch of the tribe.

DOTAKU (BELL). *Yayoi Period.*

Even if we had no idea of what these objects represented, we would have to call them bronze bells (*dotaku*) because of their shape. Most experts agree that they were used to make sounds, but do not know in what circumstances or how they were used. The bells consistently have the same shapes, crested conelike trunks with symmetrical geometric designs of spiraling volutes. Bells of later periods do away with such uniform decoration and become more realistic, with scenes of birds, animals, fishing and hunting — scenes reminiscent of daily life. In any case, they must have been used as bells and, like similar objects found during the Chinese Fighting Kingdoms and Korean periods, from which they probably derive, they also might have served in magical rituals.

Dotaku (*bell*)
Second-third century; Yayoi period
Bronze; height, 19"; found at Sumiyoshi-cho,
Higashinada, Kobe.

HEAD ORNAMENT. *Kofun Period.*

This ornament is made up of two layers of gilt bronze. A lightly-engraved decorative piece, shaped hemispherically for headwear, at one time must have held a plume, which would have indicated the rank of the bearer. Like many other similar Korean works of the period, it may have been worn, skull-cap fashion, under a crown adorned with gilt trimmings and stones (*magatama*). The piece was found among the funerary trappings of a Funayama mound tomb and has been dated to the fifth century A.D., the so-called Kofun period or the period of the "ancient tombs" (fourth to sixth century A.D.). Through contacts with the Asiatic continent, and particularly the Korean peninsula, the bronze and iron cultures of this period flourished in Japan.

HANIWA: BUST OF AN ARMORED MAN. *Kofun Period.*

Almost all archaic art in Japan is sculptural and fully represents the civilization of this early period. Even if the symbolic ritual and magical purposes of the figures remain obscure, they are nonetheless sensitive monu-

KOREA OR JAPAN
Head ornament
Fifth century A.D. Kofun period
Gilt bronze; height, 6 5/16";
classified among national treasures.

Haniwa: bust of an armored man
Sixth century. Kofun period
Terra-cotta bust; height, 25 2/3";
found at Kami-chujo, Kumagaya.
Classified among national treasures.

ments of expression. This young warrior is important for two reasons: as an esthetic object and as documentation. It belongs to a type of terra cottas called *haniwa* which literally means circle or cylinder of clay. It was originally employed (fourth century A.D.) as a protective palisade-like structure around tombs to keep the earth from sliding or even to keep away evil spirits. The figure is akin to the Japanese warriors of the Korean expeditions (fifth century) whose helmets, breastplates and swords are symbols of military power. All haniwa figures look like this, with ears, nose and hair modeled in relief. The eyes are empty, the eyebrows are slightly raised and the mouth, a mere slit in the clay, looks as if it had been wounded. Female haniwas are often overwhelming representations in which the face becomes an extraordinary example of ideal beauty.

71

GIGAKU MASK. *Asuka Period.*

Wooden ceremonial masks were used for sacred and profane dances in monasteries and in imperial courts. They endowed the dance (*gigaku*) with a particular meaning. They represent divinities, bodhisattvas, men, women and birds. The faces of human beings are curiously Occidental and never Oriental. The mask in the illustration was used in some important event for a noble from Wu and its character is underscored by its emphatic features and crown. Masks were brought from China (500–700 A.D.) where they were used in religious Buddhist ceremonies and in court dances during the Sui dynasty (589–618). They are different from the No drama masks in that they are completely round and cover the whole face and part of the head. Also unlike the No masks, which observe more closely the human features, these are markedly caricatural and grotesque. The example illustrated overwhelms us with its arrogant vitality and its intense, intelligent stare.

Gigaku mask: Goko (Prince of Wu)
Seventh century. Asuka period
Colored wood; height, 11 5/16",
width 8 1/3"; from the Horyuji treasury.

Seated Buddha
Seventh century. Asuka period
Gold-plated copper; height, 13 3/8";
from the Horyuji treasury.
Classified among national treasures.

SEATED BUDDHA. *Asuka Period.*

In China, sculpture is not considered an art like painting and certain handcrafts. In Japan, however, it came to be revered because of the work of one man, Tori Busshi, who was celebrated for his three Buddhas in the Horyu Temple's Hall of Gold (*Kondo*) done in 623 A.D. We see here a seated Buddha performing a gesture (*mudra*) of assurance (*abhaya mudra*). It dates from the Asuka period (552–645), the time when the first Buddhas were introduced into Japan along with the religion. This example is Indian in religious iconography, Chinese in style of drapery and Korean in temperament. The robe which expands at the bottom like a hoof makes us think that it derives from Chinese religious statuary of the Northern Wei dynasty (386–534 A.D.) and recalls the Horyuji Buddha.

DETAIL OF BUDDHIST BANNER. *Asuka Period.*

The introduction of Buddhism into Japan in 538 or 552 A.D. marked the beginning of a new era in artistic expression. Most painting, sculpture and handcrafts were used in celebration of the new religion. Banners or standards (*ban*), made up of bands of cloth or metal plates, were sometimes employed in ceremonial rites. The example illustrated is a small section of a gilt-bronze standard 10 feet high. The figures in the design have been grooved with fine lines which were at one time filled with enamel. A lateral floral decoration encloses the *apsara* who are flying celestial nymphs, considered by ancient Indian mythology as divinities of nature and fertility and experts at converting ascetics through their beauty. They were adopted into the Buddhist pantheon as *deva* or spiritual beings subject to the cycle of birth and rebirth (*samsara*) and were often represented flying in couples with their draperies fluttering like tongues of flames.

VASE WITH LID. *Nara Period.*   *p. 76*

This object was excavated in 1907 from an ancient tomb in the city of Ibaraki and belongs to a characteristic type of glazed ceramic known in China as *san-ts'ai* (*sansai* in Japan) or "three colors." The technique made use of glazes with a lead base which were baked at low temperatures. Western in origin, the technique spread into China in the early centuries of the Christian era through Central Asia and Persia. Its color array, which may or may not respect the name "three colors," goes from a brown yellow to an intense green and its design can be abstract or figurative. Glazed earthware spread from China over all the Far East, including the "three-color" and the "egg-and-spinach" or spotted types. For a long time it was thought that the Japanese examples came from China but recent investigation of clays and glazes has proved that they were made in local kilns in the eighth century A.D. They are called *Nara-sansai* which indicates the period in which Nara was the capital of Japan. The globular vase illustrated here was perhaps a crematory urn. The flame (*hoshu*) or the lid knob fortunately still preserves the dazzling colors with which the vase was originally covered. Typical is the decoration of horizontal lines which are incised in the clay before it has been smoothed down on the lathe.

Detail of a Buddhist banner (ban)
Seventh century A.D. Asuka period
Gilt bronze; detail from a group of
sixteen plates; 15 3/4″ × 4 3/4″.
Classified among national treasures.

CREMATORY URN. *Nara Period.*   *p. 76*

The spreading of the practice of cremation, introduced into Japan with Buddhism, prompted the manufacture of numerous crematory urns, made in wood, ceramic or metal, the first examples of which date to the beginning of the eighth century A.D. This globular receptacle has a lid with the characteristic knob or "flame" (*hoshu*), and a shape similar to the other crematory urn reproduced on this page. Made of bronze, finished on the lathe, gilded, today it is covered with a greenish patina. It was found in 1945 during an excavation near the ruins of a Buddhist temple near Nara.

Detail of Buddhist banner
(kanjo-ban)
Seventh-eighth century. Asuka-Nara period
Gilt bronze; height, 217 1/2";
from the Horyuji.
Classified among national treasures.

DETAIL OF BUDDHIST BANNER. *Asuka-Nara Period.*

A series of bronze plates similar to those in the illustration on page 74 form this banner which is held together at the top by a bronze plate. From this hangs a series of chains with filigree decoration. The photograph cannot give a good idea of the workmanship and arabesque decoration of the piece which is 6 feet long. We do not know when the work was made, but it is included in the Horyuji inventories of 737. According to religious tradition, the faithful who brushed their head against the chains would obtain a state of grace and then could go through the ceremony of aspersion or the *kanjo* which gave the name of *kanjo-ban* to this important liturgical instrument.

Vase with lid
Beginning of the eighth century.
Nara period. Glazed ceramic;
height, 6 1/4", maximum diameter 8 1/4".
Classified among national treasures.

Crematory urn
Middle eighth century A.D. Nara period
Gilt bronze; height, 7 3/4",
maximum diameter 8 1/4".

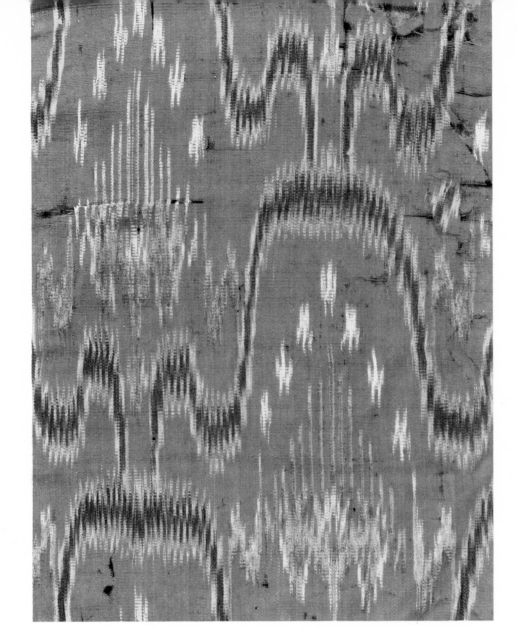

Detail of banner (ban)
Seventh century A.D. Asuka period.
Silk; total length about 120", width
13". From Horyuji, and classified
among national treasures.

DETAIL OF A BANNER (BAN). *Asuka Period.*

Textiles have been popular in Japan for 2000 years and fragments of hemp and silk this old are still extant. The *Wei-shu,* a Chinese chronicle, tells us that in the third century A.D. the Japanese were cultivating the silkworm and that a Japanese sovereign had sent Korean Chinese governors a gift of tapestries named *chin,* meaning "brocades." The *Nihon-shoki,* a Japanese text of 720 A.D., also refers to the development of textiles in Japan because of contributions made by Korean immigrant craftsmen who had introduced techniques of weaving and tinting. After the beginning of Buddhism in the sixth century, contacts with Korea and China intensified and produced a noticeable improvement in textiles. The Japanese began to use tapestries and banners in religious liturgy as decoration and started working them in the same techniques used by craftsmen on the mainland. The treasure of Horyuji of Nara, one of the oldest Buddhist temples in Japan, still has numerous banners intact. The design illustrated here is patterned with recurrent abstract motifs which are probably stylized human figures. The chest

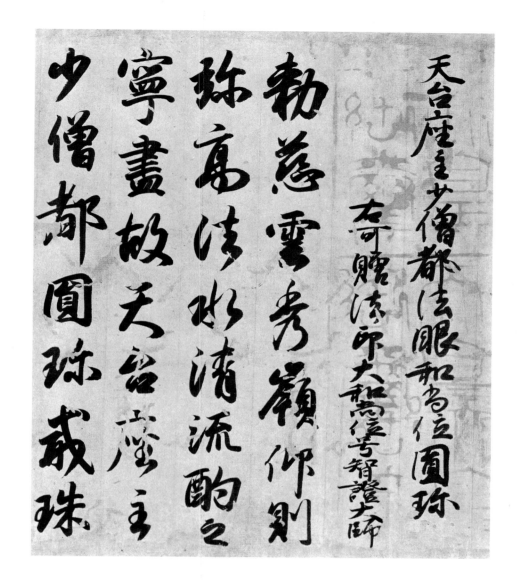

and extremities are rendered in violent yellow-edged lines and the blue-and-green head is crowned with a white-marked diadem. This work bears a resemblance to the Indonesian *ikat*, the technique of which is very similar. The *ikat* fabrics have designs which are repeated and silhouetted against a red background.

In Japan this technique is known as *tategasuri;* the woof is filled with a certain number of vertical threads or double the number of threads in the warp.

ONO NO MICHIKAZE
894–966
Imperial Rescript for the monk Enchin (927)
(*Enchin Shingo Chokusho*)
Heian period
Black-ink calligraphy. Colored paper scroll; 11 1/4″ × 62 4/5″. The manuscript is the work of Ono no Michikaze (894–966), an expert calligrapher of the imperial chancelry who, with Fujiwara no Sukemasa (944–998) and Fujiwara no Yukinari (972–1027), is known as one of the *sanseki,* the so-called "triumvirates" of calligraphy in the Heian period (794–1185). Classified among the national treasures.

ONO NO MICHIKAZE.   *Imperial Rescript for the Monk Enchin.*
This document (*Enchin Shingo Chokusho*) is the copy of an imperial rescript, drafted in 927. It posthumously conferred on the monk Enchin (814–890), a well-known prelate of the Buddhist sect of Tendai, the title of Chisho Daishi. Countersigned by the minister with his private seal, the

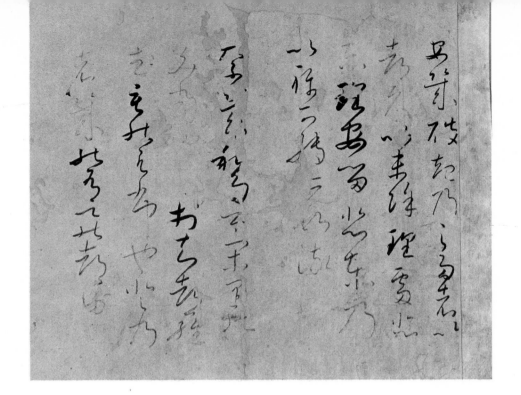

ONO NO MICHIKAZE(?)
Poetic text
(*Akihagi-jo*)
Heian Period
Black-ink calligraphy.
Scroll of colored paper; 9 1/2″ × 369 1/4″.
Classified as a national treasure.

original was usually kept in the imperial archives; a copy was sent to the temple where the person being honored held a high position. The importance of the document is not only of an historical nature (the original rescript has been lost), it also is of major artistic value, offering one of the most exemplary instances of ancient Japanese calligraphy. It is a known fact Japan took ideographic and esthetic writing standards from China, but the Japanese adapted the graphic signs to their own uses. In this case, the writing is full in body, executed in the so-called "printed" style and the signs are formed in a conspicuously elegant and simple manner.

ONO NO MICHIKAZE(?). *Poetic Text.*
This calligraphic essay, part of a poetry anthology scroll (*Akihagi-jo*) more than 25 feet long, is also attributed to Ono no Michikaze. The writing is naturally much different from the preceding example. This is not an official document, but a manuscript for private use. The forms have the fluidity of handwriting, and the simplification of the ideograms produce an unlabored effect. We can observe a noticeable attempt to move away from rigid ideography toward free-form writing. Such an abbreviation of shapes reflects in certain ways the same process that led to the elaboration of the syllabic alphabet (*hiragana*).

HATA NO CHITEI(?). *Illustrated Biography of Shotoku Taishi.*
This work illustrates the gradual evolution of Japanese painting from the period of pure imitation of mainland art to the development of an auton-

HATA NO CHITEI(?)
Heian period
Illustrated biography of Shotoku Taishi
(*Shotoku Taishi Eden*) (1069)
Detail.
Panels from a series of screens;
74 1/2″ × 108 1/2″
Classified among the national treasures.
Opposite: *The Arrival of Prince Asa.*

omous national style. This led to the splendid accomplishments of the Yamato-e school or the "painting of Yamato" as it was called in ancient Japanese. The name was used to distinguish this art from Chinese-influenced painting, known as *Kara-e* or *Kanga*. The plate on page 81 echoes in composition and the treatment of the figures, faces and colors a pronounced Chinese influence. The plate on page 83, on the other hand, presents a scene in which not one detail suggests anything but the typical Japanese style, especially in the construction of the scene, the placing of the figures and their attitudes and dress. With this work, Japanese art, in a certain sense, proves that it is well aware of the details of everyday life, its habits and customs. Naturally, genre painting was the first to abandon the classical canons of Chinese art in order to meet its particular needs. Its subject matter included scenes of annual festivities, stories of sanctuaries and temples, biographies of illustrious men and romantic anecdotes. They were executed on mural panels, screens, movable walls, manuscripts and scrolls. This typical Yamato painting shows a bird's-eye perspective, buildings seen at an angle without roofs or ceilings so that the viewer can look in and observe the sumptuous interiors where the actions take place. Shotoku Taishi (573–622) was a prince who, according to tradition, gave his country its first written laws and patronized Buddhism, elevating it almost to the rank of a state religion. Originally, the biographical series of paintings decorated a pavilion of Horyuji. According to reports of the time, the works were executed between the second and the fifth month of 1068 by the painter Hata no Chitei. In 1788 they were moved from their original site and were mounted on a five-panel screen. The *Shotoku Taishi Denreki*, a "biography of Prince Shotoku" compiled in 917 by Fujiwara Kanesuke, served as a source of themes. The paintings represent 58 scenes from the life of the celebrated statesman. They are not, however, distributed in chronological order. Page 83 shows the birth of the prince and page 81 refers to a later date when the prince pays a visit to the Korean prince Asa. Although it has been restored several times, it is still a major work and offers one of the best-known and characteristic illustrated biographies of early Yamato-e compositions.

TWO 'ARHATS'. *From the 'Juroku Rakan' Series.*   *pp. 84–85*
These plates illustrate two *arhats* (in Japanese *rakan*), Asita Sonja and Bajarahottara Sonja respectively, two personages of lofty spirituality who attained enlightenment through meditation and the close observance of

HATA NO CHITEI
Illustrated biography of Shotoku Taishi.
Detail: *Birth of the Prince.*

Two Arhats
From the series "The Sixteen Arhats" (*Juroku Rakan*). Second half of the eleventh century. Heian period Kakemono painted in colors on silk: each is 38 1/4″ × 20 1/2″. Classified among the national treasures.

Buddha's precepts. Established in China during the T'ang period (618–906), Buddhist iconography exalted between 16 and 18 of these spiritual beings who renounced nirvana to stay on Earth and protect the Buddhist law. These highly edifying paintings were widely dispersed through Japan, where they became a major cult in the Zen monasteries. The Zen doctrine, in fact, exalted the ideal of the *arhat* as a symbol of man who attains salvation through his own means. These paintings, however, date from before the introduction of Zen into Japan and belong to the early cultist attempts of the patriarchs. A few other representations had already been executed in the eighth century on the mural paintings of the Joryuji golden hall. But the iconography of the "sixteen" seems to have been introduced in Japan

only in 987 by the monk Chonen, and it appears that they were first represented under Chinese influence in the eleventh century.

The two illustrated examples are from a series of 16 hanging scrolls and are among the oldest of this subject preserved. They show obvious Chinese influence in the treatment of the faces and the costume details, which are intended to create an exotic atmosphere of great distance. The figures are seen in attitudes of prayer and are placed between temples and mountains. The angle of the veranda is a bold translation from the architectonic compositions of the Yamato-e style which at this time was freeing itself from Chinese influence.

THE BODHISATTVA SAMANTABHADRA. *Heian Period.*

Riding a white elephant on a canopy of lotus, Fugen, Bosatsu, the Bodhisattva Samantabhadra, is descending to Earth from the Oriental Paradise in order to protect the devout of the "Sutra of the Lotus of Good Law" (*Saddharma-pundarika sutra*). He is showered with flowers and lotus petals in a scene of spiritual serenity. The figure of the Bodhisattva, symbol of compassion and pity, has renounced nirvana so that he can continue to save creatures on Earth. As the Buddhist faith became progressively humanized, this Bodhisattva became the ideal of Japanese Buddhism and one of the favorite themes of religious art. In the twelfth century, Buddhist painting reached an apex of perfection in Japan, uniting a delicacy of craftsmanship with a solemnity of style and a delicacy of taste which had deeply pervaded the culture. The sacred icons of the sutra of the lotus cult are conspicuously feminine. Their text is devoted to the faith and salvation of women. The illustrated figure, which is one of the most celebrated Bodhisattvas among the women of the Heian court (794–1185), is markedly effeminate in the delicacy of her face, the soft lines of her body and her gossamer clothing and profusion of jewels. We get a three-quarter view of the figure, symbolizing that the figure is an intermediary between Buddha and earthly beings.

THE 'PEACOCK KING' (KUJAKU–MYOO). *Heian Period.*   p. 88

Kujaku-myoo (*Mahamayura-vidyaraja* in Sanskrit) is the "peacock king" or the deification of the bird which preys on serpents. Belief would have it that in an earlier life Buddha was transformed into a peacock and managed, in this disguise, to make water spring miraculously from a rock. Buddhism elevated the peacock (*mayura*) to the rank of one of the "great king protectors" of the law and turned the figure into a benevolent divinity, endowed with the powers of ending natural calamities. The Shingon Buddhist sect spread the cult through Japan in the Heian period (794–1185). A miracle is tied up with the origins of the cult. In 908, the monk Seiho is supposed to have implored for rain before an image of this divinity in the imperial palace, and soon a long drought ended. Religious iconography prescribed a "strict canon for *Kujaku-myoo* images and altars" (the *Daikujakumyoo Gazo Danjo Giki*) and the painting illustrated here sticks closely to it. The four-armed divinity — symbol of multiple powers — is seated with crossed legs on a lotus flower carried aback a wingspread peacock. Each hand holds an emblem: a lotus flower, pomegranate, orange, peacock-tail feather. In the background, there are a multi-colored halo and a large green gilt nimbus that echoes the design of the feather and the shape of the tail. Four small liturgical jars rest on lotus pedestals and each contains a lotus blossom out of which rises the sacred symbol of lightning, the *vajra*. The image is rigidly frontal. The description of the goldware and

86

Bodhisattva Samantabhadra (*Fugen Bosatsu*)
First half of the twelfth century.
Heian period
Kakemono painted in colors on silk: 63 1/2″ × 29 1/2″.
Classified among the national treasures.
Right: Detail

The "Peacock King" (Kujaku-myoo)
First half of the twelfth century.
Heian period
Kakemono painted in colors on silk;
59 1/2" × 39 1/2".
Classified among the national treasures.

clothing is precious and the characterization of the divinity's face is Central Asian in taste. But the fineness of design and the sumptuous polychromy are without a doubt Japanese. Nothing mars the plane by suggesting volume or space.

BODHISATTVA AKASAGARBHA. *Heian Period.*

The *Akasagarbha Bodhisattva* (*Kokuzo Basatsu* in Japanese) is the personification of incommensurable wisdom and infinite sagacity. He was venerated as patron and precursor of human intelligence. In the Heian period (794–1185), the Buddhist sect of Shingon considered him a carrier of happiness and liked to represent him seated on a lotus throne atop the Sumeru mountain. Regarded as a moon symbol *par excellence,* the figure was, according to iconographical use, circumscribed in a large halo. The composition is highly intellectual and stylistically severe. This painting is one of the few sacred images used for ritual purposes in the Shingon temples that have been preserved. Executed in intense colors, it is adorned in a miniature-like technique with golden and silver leaves which create a particularly decorative effect. Although of small size, the work is indeed on a grand scale.

Bodhisattva Akasagarbha
(*Kokuzo Bosatsu*)
Middle of the twelfth century.
Heian period.
Detail
Kakemono painted in colors on silk;
52 1/2" × 33 1/4".
Classified national treasure.

89

Cosmetic box
Twelfth century. Heian period
Lacquered wood with mother-of-pearl encrustations and gold inlays; height, 5″, length 12″, width 9″. Classified among the national treasures.

Trunk
Twelfth century. Heian period
Lacquered wood with mother-of-pearl encrustations; height, 23 1/2″, width 27″, length 37″. From the treasure of Horyuji. Classified among the national treasures.

COSMETIC BOX. *Heian Period.*

A design of wheels with spokes partially immersed in water decorates the outside of this precious box from the late Heian period (794–1185). It is certainly one of the most splendid lacquer works of Japanese art. The wheels are encrusted with mother-of-pearl and inlaid with thin gold leaf on lacquer covered with gold dust. Also inlaid are gold threads that make up a *ryusu-imon* or "flowing water" design giving a suggestion of waves. It has been conjectured that the pattern was inspired from the custom of immersing cart wheels into the river in order to avoid overheating the wheels and to dry-up of the wood fibers after a long period in the beating sun. But ancient literature has also taught us that defective wheels were thrown into river beds. The inside of the box is covered with designs of flowers, birds and butterflies executed in *maki-e* with gold and silver dust.

TRUNK. *Heian Period.*

This small six-legged trunk is a Chinese type (Japanese trunks are legless) and is wrought in wood, lacquered black and encrusted with large and small mother-of-pearl medallions representing phoenixes (*feng* in Chinese). Chinese legend made these mythical birds with brilliant plumage into symbols of good fortune. The technique for making encrustations with shells (*raden* in Japanese) probably originated in Southern Asia, but had been used in China since the T'ang period (618–906), and it was introduced into Japan in the Nara period (645–794). From then on, the art of lacquer was widely practiced in Japan and works were decorated with encrustations, inlays and painting. Decorating in *maki-e* (sprinkled painting) consisted typically of making designs in liquid lacquer amalgamated with vegetable and mineral colors over which a leafing of gold or silver was spread. Fused with the *raden,* the *maki-e* technique blended pearl-like reflections of the shells with gold and silver dust executed in the *maki-e* technique.

LOTUS SUTRA ON A FAN. *Heian Period.*   *p. 93*

In Japan during the late Heian period, other works besides sacred objects were made for religious celebrations or for spiritual edification. There were, for example, illuminated manuscripts executed on scrolls or on fan-shaped paper sheets, illustrating for the most part the sutra or canonical Buddhist texts. We find in them the first synthesis between calligraphy and painting which gave Japanese art in the following centuries its remarkable originality. Unlike classical religious painting, whose subjects are determined by iconography, this type of work gradually liberated itself from ritualistic limits and changed into a painting of religious exegesis in which sacred elements and truths of faith flourished even in scenes of a profane subject matter. The process was made easier by the fact that in many cases the artists who did these works were not monk painters, but laymen artists who were interested in illustrating religious texts or simply in copying parts of sacred designs. It has been suggested that the original for this work was a black-and-white wood print which the artist had only to color. Sometimes the subject was a celestial vision or a scene of private devotion, and often an episode from contemporary life having no connection whatsoever with the sacred text. Gold and silver dust specks were then sprinkled on the miniatures. The paintings on fan-shaped paper indicated a conspicuous preference for secular scenes rather than religious ideas and contemplative images. The text illustrated here was a fan-shaped page from a copybook. Each page is made up of 24 lines with 18 ideograms each. Following the form of the fan, the characters gradually get smaller toward the bottom. The painting is in pure *Yamato-e* style and the plate depicts scenes of craftsman activities.

Lotus sutra on a fan
(*Semmen Hokke-kyo Sasshi*)
Second half of the twelfth century. Heian period. Painted in colors and black-ink calligraphy on paper; height 10″, width 19 1/2″. Classified among the national treasures.

VASE WITH LOTUS PETALS. *Heian Period.* p. 94

Before the end of the Heian period (794–1185) glazing with lead-based varnishes called "three colors" fell into disuse and was replaced by the hard feldspar or the so-called "ash" glazings obtained with vegetable carbons for colors varying from green to brown. Preferred for their rustic beauty, these terra cottas took on the appearance of the ancient *sue* ceramics of the fourth and fifth centuries A.D. and subsequently acquired a wide renown, owing to the masters of the tea ceremonies who named them "mountain tea cups" or *yamachawan*. Between the Heian and Kamakura periods (1185–1333), the *tokonabe* ceramics came into vogue. They were known for their raw materials containing glass fragments which melted during the firing and produced the first layer of glazing. Then the outside was sprinkled with a black smoke and crystalline mixture which intensified the brown color of the firing. The *tokonabe* vases were frequently used for ritual burials of Buddhist texts in the so-called "sutra" mounds. The illustrated example was excavated in 1918, in the city of Numazu, along with a copper case for sacred books and a mirror, both from the Heian-Kamakura period. Finding the objects together made it possible to date them all to the second half of the twelfth century. Like many *tokonabe* ceramics, this piece was not worked on a lathe but made from a circular form in three separate parts which were fitted together with punchings. The joining lines between the bottom and the belly, and the belly and the shoulder, are still visible. This particular

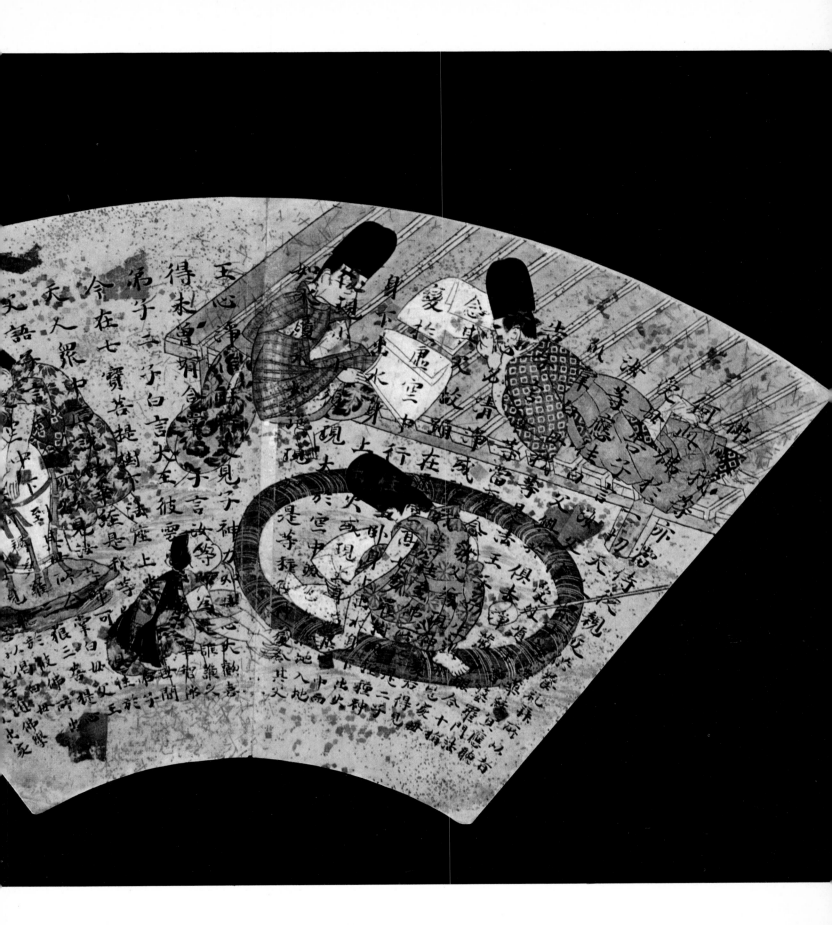

Vase with lotus petals
Second half of the twelfth century.
Heian period
Glazed earthware; height 16 1/2".

technique was difficult because of the friable nature of the materials and the complicated forms. The crudely incised decoration on the upper part of the vase was formed by a double series of semicircles or stylized lotus petals between horizontal lines.

HELL SCROLLS (JIGOKU ZOSHI). *Kamakura Period.*

Following the long civil wars, calamities and poverty which struck Japan during the Kamakura period (1185–1333), religious thought took on a pessimistic vision and the sense that all wrongs had to be atoned for. By way of warning, sacred art multiplied representations of scenes of final justice and infernal punishment described by the canonical texts. Some scrolls illustrated in extreme detail the torments and anguish of the Eight Hells. The one illustrated is the fire cloud. Perennial flames burn the sinners who have been guilty of a life of heavy drinking or who watered down wine or invited others to drink against their will, as well as those who made monks drunk and then made fun of them. Unyielding monsters push the damned into the inferno; long red flames create a scene of horrifying beauty in impetuous linear rhythms.

Hell scrolls (Jigoku Zoshi)
End of the twelfth century.
Kamakura period
Makimon painted in colors on paper;
10 3/8" × 96".
Classified among national treasures.

Liturgical object (kongo-ban)
Twelfth century. Heian period
Gilt bronze;
height 16 1/2", maximum diameter 9 1/2",
minimum 3/4".
Important national treasure.

LITURGICAL OBJECT.   *Heian Period.*

Used for religious purposes by Buddhists, this dish was placed in the center of the altar during services. An object of very pure symbolism, its lobed shape represents in a stylized manner the symbol of lightning (*vajra* in Sanskrit, *kongo* in Japanese, hence the name *kongo-ban* given the work). The design, set off by gilt edges, was executed with a floral motif in friezes along the raised edge. There are three symmetrical lotus plants in the center of the dish.

SCROLLS FROM THE HISTORY OF THE HEIJI ERA.   *Kamakura Period.*

An important chapter in the history of *Yamato-e* was marked by the appearance of secular book illustrations, especially of the *monogatari-e* which illustrate historical romances (*monogatari*). The illustrations were for books (*toji-hon,* bound books) and scrolls which unwound horizontally (*makimon, emaki* or *ekotoba*). Among the latter are the famous scrolls of *Heiji Monogatari* (The Story of the Heiji). It is a long story of the struggles in Kyoto in the second half of the twelfth century to find a successor to the throne. There are many representations of this event, which is known as the transfer of the imperial family to Rokuhara. It is made up of fifteen sheets and shows the first four chapters of the story, scenes of which are reproduced here in detail illustrations. The upper plate shows the Emperor Nijo, who, after having been confined to a wing of the imperial palace by the

Scrolls from the history of the Heiji era
Thirteenth century. Kamakura period
Details. Color paintings on paper;
382" × 17".
Classified among the national treasures.

Above: *The Emperor Bestirs Himself to Leave the Palace Disguised as a Woman.*
Right: *The Raiding of the Imperial Palace.*
Pages 98–99: *The Emperor's Retinue Hastens to Leave the Palace.*

96

mutinous troops led by Minmoto Yoshitomo, flees in the disguise of a woman of the court and hides in the residence of Taira no Kiyomoro at Rokuhara. In the lower plate, Fujiwara Nobuyori, one of the principal allies of Yoshitomo in the mutiny, is astonished when he learns of the Emperor's escape and uselessly has the imperial palace searched. In the third plate, the court nobles learn that the Emperor is already in Rokuhara and prepare to go after him.

The style of the composition is of major interest, for it marks one of the high points of narrative painting in the Kamakura period for the elegance of its decorative line and the harmony of its colors. The mastery and precision of the design make the work a precious document of the customs of the period: the types of clothing and armor, the ox-drawn, covered carts with large spoked wheels, the architecture and the interiors of the sumptuous residences. It should be noted that landscape is completely missing from this work and that the individual scenes are composed of figure groups. Though conventional, the figures are highly characterized. The dark and lively colors stand out against a neutral background. Its author is uncertain but some experts attribute the work to Sumiyoshi Keion, a painter who is supposed to have exercised considerable influence on the art of Tosa.

STORY OF THE SANCTUARY OF KITANO TENJIN. *Kamakura Period.* This scene represents the madness of a woman in the court of the Emperor Toba (1103–1156). She had been punished by a divinity for having slandered the monk Ajari Ninshun, a saintly man. The monk had retired to a monastery, but was called to exorcise the evil spirits possessing the miserable woman. The story (*Kitano Tenjin Engi*) illustrates one of the many miraculous episodes that are attributed to Tenjin, the statesman and intellectual Sugawar no Michizane (845–903), who became known as a saintly master of calligraphy and wisdom. During the second half of the ninth century, when the Fujiwara were monopolizing the administrative power of the imperial court, Michizane, acting as minister and consul, repeatedly attempted to weaken the power of the ambitious family. He fell, however, into disgrace with the emperor and, because of unjust accusations, was exiled to Dazaifu on the distant island of Kyushu, where he probably died. Upon his death calamities of every sort struck the country and lightning hit the imperial palace. These ill-starred events were interpreted as signs of a celestial vendetta. A sanctuary was erected to the memory of Michizane. It was called the Kitano Tenjin and is currently known as the Tenmangu of Kyoto. Various stories of miracles have been linked with this sacred place of medieval shintoism. Similar works of Buddhism come to mind, principally a particular type of *engi-e,* paintings which illustrated edifying legends on temples and miraculous episodes of Buddhist divinities or sanctified monks. Numerous *Tenjin Engi* were illustrated in the *Yamato-e* style. The one reproduced here is part of a scroll showing representations taken from a series kept originally in Tenmangu. They are known as the "book of Koan" which comes from the name of their period (1278–1288). Unlike other *Tenjin Engi,* the paintings present a design of extreme finesse. Color is used as an accessory element, but integrated into the image.

Story of the Sanctuary of Kitano Tenjin (Kitano Tenjin Engi)
Second half of the thirteenth century. Kamakura period
Detail of a scroll painted with color on paper;
11 7/8" × 101".
Classified among important national treasures.

STATUE OF ONE OF THE 'TWELVE DIVINE GUARDIANS' (JUNI SHINSHO). *Kamakura Period.*

This statue represents one of the sentinels who guard Yakushi Norai (*Bhaisajyaguru* in Sanskrit), Buddha the Healer. Equal in rank to the "heavenly kings," these guards carried out the duty of protecting the faith from evil spirits and enemies of the Law. A specific iconographical type in Buddhist art, these figures have a terrifying and merciless look that expresses the unflagging zeal with which they work. Their overwhelming attitudes and the menacing faces are supposed to frighten off evil spirits and to turn them from attack. In the Yakush iconography, Buddha of medicine often appears, flanked by two bodhisattvas, Nikko Bosatsu (*Suryaprabhasa* in Sanskrit), meaning "solar light," and Gakko Bosatsu (*Candraprabha* in Sanskrit), meaning "moonlight." They are personifications of day and night. Similarly, the 12 *shinsho* personify and preside over the 12 divisions of a day for two hours each, and they all have on their head one of the 12 animals of the zodiac that in ancient astrology referred not only to the month but also to the day and to the hour.

The statue is carved in cypress wood, a rarity in Japanese sculpture which is generally made of sandalwood. A sense of indomitable force springs from the figure as he is on the verge of unsheathing his sword. His wrinkled-up nose, beetled brows, narrow lips, threatening eyes and flame-like hair give him an appearance of horror. Although heavy, the sculpture's style is still sober and prefigures the exuberant inventions of the late Kamakura period (1850–1333). From this, we can date this work to the thirteenth century.

Statue of one of the
"Twelve Divine Guardians"
(Juni Shinsho)
Thirteenth century. Kamakura period
Detail. Wood; height 31".
Work is classified among important
national treasures.

PORTRAIT OF MINAMOTO NO YORITOMO. *Kamakura Period.*

p. 104

Without any knowledge of Japanese sculpture whatsoever, the viewer immediately feels its impact. Its message is clear because it is expressed in comprehensive gestures according to our common understanding of sensitive

Portrait of Minamoto no Yoritomo
Thirteenth century. Kamakura period
Colored wood; height 28″. Classified among
important national treasures.

formal beauty and of the abstract thought that it can signify. It is therefore easy to intuit the ideal force of the figure of Minamoto no Yoritomo, a very important founder of the Kamakura dynasty (1185–1333) which takes its name from *bakufuk,* a type of military governor (originally meaning "governor of the tent") and the name of the new capital. This portrait may symbolize the intellectual force and the power of will that were synthesized in Yoritomo. His hands and feet disappear into the summary shape of the wooden block out of which they have been carved, and the overriding form suggests a strong unity of character. The legs thrust angularly forward with a strong visual impact. The bust is rigid with pride and force and the clothes are solemn in their sacred poverty. The head emerges from under the ceremonial headgear that rises like a flame.

督王法藥

毘阿旅里帝婆婆哥

舍人愛染法師

馬名クケム

丁巳日死

Page from a veterinary treatise
(circa 1267) (*Bai Zoshi*)
Kamakura period
Painted scroll on paper; 29 1/2″ × 244″.
Classified among important
national treasures.

PAGE FROM A VETERINARY TREATISE. *Kamakura Period.*

A type of Yamato painting specialized in illustrations of scientific subjects, especially in veterinary medicine (*Bai Zoshi*). Our illustration is a page from a book about two monks who are veterinarian specialists in the treatment of horses. One monk, Io Koraku, seated near a groom and a horse in a stall, was well known for his medical research and studies. We see Yakush, the Buddha of medicine (*Bhaisajyaguru* in Sanskrit), in a circle above. It was customary in works of this type to list in the upper left corner names of grooms, horses, horse masters and magic therapeutic formulas. On the other pages are illustrated the 17 types of herbs which were a major source of study for veterinarians of the period.

ILLUSTRATIONS OF TENGU (TENGU ZOSHI). *Kamakura Period.*

In Yamato painting one of the subjects was a merciless criticism leveled at certain clerics who led a worldly life and agitated for various political factions. The *tengu zoshi* were ferociously satiric and continued the tradition of the *engi-e* or illustrations of legends on temple walls created with irony and bitterness. The monks in the great temples sometimes led scandalous lives and had completely lost their faith. They were likened to the *tengu,* the seven types of evil spirits who were, according to ancient legend, responsible for great natural calamities.

This illustration is from a scroll which narrates the story of three major Japanese monasteries. The scene shows a group of monks and their faithful followers held at bay before a sacred area by a monk who is armed with a staff. Two people are dancing on the balustraded platform.

Illustrations of Tengu
(*Tengu Zoshi*)
End of the thirteenth century. Kamakura period. Detail. Pair of emakimono painted with colors on paper; 11 1/2" × 429 1/2" each. Classified among important national treasures.

HOGEN EN'I
Illustrated Biography of the
Monk Ippen (1299)
(*Ippen Shonin Eden*)
Kamakura Period
Scroll painted with colors on paper;
15 1/2" × 320 1/2".

HOGEN EN'I. *Illustrated Biography of the Monk Ippen.*
Seventh in a series of 12 scrolls, this work illustrates the life and work of
the monk Ippen (1239–1289). As founder of Ji-shu, a sect of Buddhism,
Ippen propagated his faith in the salvation of Japan through the merciful
Buddha Amitabha. Ippen's biography was compiled by one of his disciples
and was illustrated by Hogen En'i, a painter who lived between the thirteenth and fourteenth centuries. The biography tells of the principal events
in the monk's life and particularly of his evangelizing work. The scrolls
were painted about ten years after Ippen's death. The artist attempted to
recreate the people and places where the monk had conducted his prose-
lytizing campaigns. Our plate shows an animated scene of city life near a
bridge that crossed the Katsura River in Kyoto, where Ippen lived. Although the figures are done in pure Japanese *Yamato-e* style, the landscape
is suggestive of Chinese works. **107**

HIDA NO KAMI KOREHISA. *The Battle of Gosannen.*

This scene represents the mercenary warrior Minamoto no Yoshiie (1039–1106) who, followed by a few knights, is galloping toward the castle of Kanazawa. Some ducks, which have taken to flight, betray the presence of hidden enemies. The *Yamato-e* tradition of illustrated stories is continued with this work. It is a tale of war or a *"gunk-monogatari,"* immortalizing the life of Minamoto no Yoshiie, who put down the rebellion of Fujiwara Take-hira and Fujiwara Iehira in the war of Gosannen (1083–1087). Commissioned by Genkei, an abbot from the Hiei-zan monastery who helped form the legends of Minamoto, the work was completed in 1347. Originally it was supposed to include from four to six scrolls, but only three are preserved. At the end of the last scroll the artist is identified as Hida no Kamai Korehisa, a painter from the school of the Kose. The horses and warriors are superbly executed, the landscape and enemies are summarily indicated, the ducks add a splendidly colored punctuation.

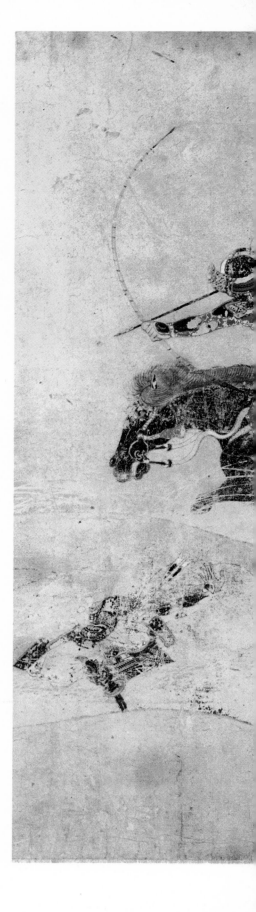

HIDA NO KAMI KOREHISA
The Battle of Gosannen
(*Gosannen Gassen Ekotoba*) (circa 1347)
Muromachi period
Detail from one of three scrolls painted on
paper;
first scroll 18 1/4″ × 756″.
Important national treasure.

KAO SHUNEN. *The Monk Hsien-Tzu.*   *p. 110*

This work introduces us to the famous type of black-ink painting, called *sumi-e* or *suiboku* in Japanese. The medium came from China at the end of the Kamakura (1185–1333) and beginning of the Muromachi period (1337–1573). Clearly inspired by Chinese Sung monochromatic painting, *Sumi* painting flourished in Japan as the importance of Zen Buddhism increased.

Kao Shunen was one of the first Zen monks to take up this art. We know little of him beyond the facts that he lived in the fourteenth century and that toward the end of the Kamakura period he went to China where he studied Ch'an Buddhism and perhaps Chinese painting in the style of Mu-ch'i.

108   Here the artist represents Hsien-tzu, a legendary hermit monk who, along

with his companion Chu-tou, fed on animals and especially crustaceans. During one of their meals he received enlightenment and was converted to Ch'an. In this printing he thanks the heavens for having caught a lobster with his little net. The painting celebrates the virtues of a simple, intimate life in nature and is executed as a sketch in a very concise and sober style with exquisite impressionistic effects.

TENNSHO SHUBUN(?). *The Hermits Han-shan and Shih-te.*
Attributed to Shubun, an artist active around the middle of the fifteenth century, this hanging scroll is one of the numerous Japanese copies of Chinese renderings of the two hermits Han-shan and Shih-te, who personify the ideal Zen men, simple, good-hearted, natural. They have the faces of innocence, they are spontaneous in their actions, pure in their thoughts. Unlike the ink paintings of China which are mere sketches, the Japanese paintings are fuller, with very refined tones of light and shade.

KAO SHUNEN
The Monk Hsien-tzu
First half of the fourteenth century.
Kamakura period
Kakemono painted with ink on paper;
34 1/2″ × 12 1/2″. Detail. Classified among important national treasures.

110

TENSHO SHUBUN(?)
The Hermits Han-shan and Shih-te
Middle of the fifteenth century.
Muromachi period
Kakemono painted with ink on paper;
39 4/5″ × 14 1/2″.
Classified among important
national treasures.

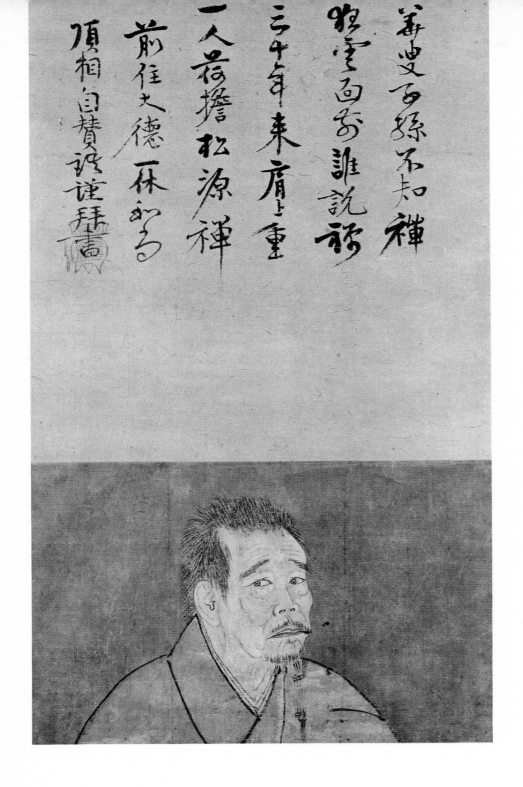

每遇百緒不知禪
粗富面乃誰說鬍
三十年来肩上重
一人荷擔松源禪
前住大德麻かる
頂相自贊況謹珪書

BOKUSAI. *Portrait of the Monk Ikkyu.*

In Japanese painting this work is one of the first examples of sketches from actual life. Unlike other portraits of monks, the painting does not present an idealized figure, but relies on the model, who had an emaciated face, thick eyebrows, a beard and penetrating eyes. Although the technique seems comparatively rudimentary, the artist knew how to catch the personality of Ikkyu (1394–1481), a famous Zen Buddhist prelate and abbot of

BOKUSAI
Portrait of the Monk Ikkyu
Second half of the fifteenth century.
Muromachi period
Kakemono painted with colors on paper;
17 1/2″ × 10 1/2″.
Classified among important
national treasures.

Daitokuji. The artist was a disciple of Ikkyu and his name was Bokusai or Shosai. Ikkyu often wrote poetry about his works. The inscription in the upper part of our painting is an imitation by Bokusai of Ikkyu's calligraphy and verse.

TOSA MITSUNOBU(?).   *History of Seikoji.*

The *Seikoji Engi,* an illustrated history of a Buddhist temple in Kyoto, described the origin of the edifice which was constructed in 1230 by Taira Sukechika in memory of his defunct mother. The temple was dedicated to Jizo Bosatsu, the bodhisattva Ksitigarbha, who was compassionate to dead people. Its foundation is related to a story. Taira Sukechika had found a bodhisattva statue and made it a cult object. The devotees of the statue obtained numerous graces. One woman whose roof had been damaged by a tempest was helped by the bodhisattva who sent some monks to help repair it. For this miracle, the bodhisattva was nicknamed "roof repairer." The plate illustrates the ruined house and the bodhisattva appearing in divine intervention.

TOSA MITSUNOBU(?)
History of Seikoji (1487)
(*Seikoji Engi*)
Muromachi period
Detail. Scroll painted with colors on paper;
13 1/5″ × 425″.
Classified among important national treasures.

113

SESSHU TOYO
1420–1506
Landscape (1495)
Muromachi period
Kakemono painted with ink on paper;
59″ × 13″.
Classified among national treasures.

SESSHU TOYO. *Landscape.*

During the Muromachi period (1337–1573), the Japanese continued to assimilate various Chinese techniques and styles, from the lively coloring of the T'ang dynasty to the ink works of the Sung. Nevertheless, the Japanese were able to develop an indigenous style of *Yamato-e*. The Japanese in this period also adopted a Chinese ink technique (*p'o-mo*), which is called *"haboku"* in Japanese. Sesshu (1420–1506), who lived for a long time in China, is one of the most celebrated Japanese practitioners of this technique. The painting illustrated here is a typical example of *haboku*. It is a landscape scroll, over 4 feet high. The technique attains an extraordinary expressive power. Mountains and sky, sketchily executed, evoke a severe sense of solitude, as if the artist wanted to suggest rather than to state. Certainly the painting is no reproduction of a specific site, but rather a combination of ideal spots which he had imagined. It is said that the artist's blacks "could suggest the five colors."

SESSHU TOYO
Winter and Autumn Landscapes
Second half of the fifteenth century.
Muromachi period
Two kakemonos painted with ink on paper;
each 18 1/2″ × 11 1/2″.
Classified among national treasures.

SESSHU TOYO. *Autumn and Winter Landscapes.*

These two landscapes by Sesshu differ from the one previously described. They represent his mature style, and were executed after he returned from the mainland, where he had studied and copied Chinese masters. The rocks in the winter landscape are sharply cut, as with a razor. The mountain, vanishing at the top, suggests infinity and the little house at the bottom looks as if it were lost in a tragic immensity of space. In this case, the *haboku* technique is not a murmur but a resounding shout. In the autumn landscape, sky fills up the scene, dominating all.

KETTLE FOR TEA WATER. *Muromachi Period.*

The spreading of the tea ceremony among all classes of Japanese in the Muromachi period (1337–1573) turned humble water kettles into one of the most appreciated types of the iron-worker's art. The main industries sprang up in Tenmyo and Ashiya. The kettle illustrated here is an example from Ashiya and it is known as a *shinnari-gama,* which means that it is a pot with a rounded bottom and a narrow mouth. Its ring-shaped handles (*kantsuki*) were given little monster marks. Still in its original state, the kettle's surface is decorated in relief with five small horses silhouetted against a landscape of hills.

Kettle for tea water (chanoyu-gama)
End of the fifteenth or beginning of sixteenth century.
Muromachi period.
Iron; height 7 1/2", diameter 12 2/5".

Lantern
Sixteenth century. Muromachi period. Bronze; height 12 2/5", upper diameter 13 4/5". The object comes from the factories of Tenmyo and was found in 1910 in the lost Buddhist temple of Chiba. Classified among the important national treasures.

LANTERN. *Muromachi Period.*

An inscription finely incised on the upper register of this lantern gives the following data: "Lantern of Hizendo donated by Ushio Hyobu Shoyu on the 28th day of the 7th month of the 19th year of Tenmon (1550). Chibadera, Ikeda, Chiba, province of Shimosa." Hexagonal in form, the lantern imitates a building with a raised roof and was cast in one piece, except for a little door. The base rests on three "cat's paws" (*neko-ashi*). The decoration on the grill includes flowering prunus trees and burgeoning bamboo. The lid has two air openings and a flamelike knob rises from the top. Its lengthy burial in the earth produced a fine bluish-green patina.

WRITING BOX (SUZURIBAKO). *Muromachi Period.*

In the Kamakura period the introduction of the techniques of *takamaki-e* and *maki-e* in relief perfected Japanese lacquer ware. Fine naturalistic compositions are designed on the black lacquer background of this writing box. A moonscape is visible on the outer lid and mountains and trees make up the decoration on the lids of the inner boxes. The landscape is very much akin to contemporaneous landscape paintings. The box usually contained ink pens, paper scrolls, brushes, a stone for blotting the ink and a small water vase.

Writing box (*suzuribako*)
Fifteenth century. Muromachi period
Lacquered wood; height 2″, length 9″, width 8 1/2″. This work is one of the finest lacquer products of the Muromachi period (1337–1573) and belonged to the *shogun* Ashikaga Yoshimasa (1435–1490).

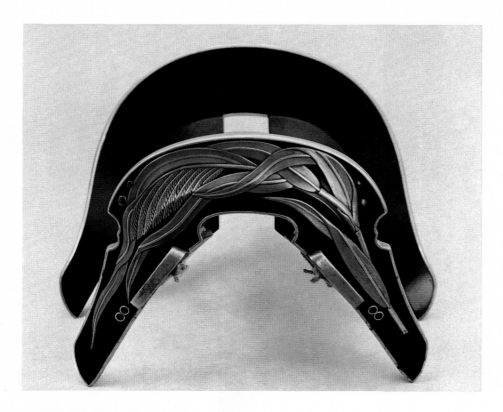

KANO EITOKU(?)
Saddle
Second half of the sixteenth century.
Momoyama period
Lacquered wood; height in front 11″,
in back 11 1/2″.

KANO EITOKU(?). *Saddle*.

The Japanese noble warriors always enjoyed elegant weapons as well as elegant trappings for their steeds. Lacquer was often used for finishing each piece, especially the saddles. We think that the saddle illustrated here belonged to Toyotomi Hideyoshi (1536–1598), who is supposed to have commissioned the celebrated painter Kano Eitoku (1543–1590) to decorate it. Lacquered in black, it has a design of stylized gilt leaves.

SILK KIMONO OF THE NUIHAKU TYPE. *Momoyama Period.*

The *kimono,* which literally means "dress," is the traditional Japanese attire for both men and women. It consists of a long ample tunic covering everything but the feet and is furnished with long sleeves and tightened at the waist by a band of material called the *shita-gime.* On top of this is the *obi,* a belt of damask silk. The *nuihaku* is a type of *kimono* worn by actors who are playing women's parts in the nō theater. From the very beginning, women, for reasons of morality, were not allowed on the stage and male actors had to perform in women's as well as men's roles. In their various parts or personifications, they wore particular types of masks and costumes. The *nuihaku* were indeed costumes which were made precisely for women. Their material was preciously decorated or embroidered with leaves; gold threads were interspersed or superimposed. (*Nuihaku* literally means superimposed.) The design was usually composed of floral motifs. The example illustrated is made up of large red and white rectangles. The decoration includes plants, festoons and little bridges. It has been embroidered with silk and gold threads and bears the poetic name of "flowers and plants from the four seasons."

Silk kimono
Second half of the sixteenth century
Momoyama period
Costume for the No theater of the
nuihaku type; height 55″,
shoulders 23 1/2″. This is one of the most
celebrated textiles of the Momoyama period
(1586–1615).

118

KANO HIDEYOURI. *Excursion to Takao.*

This work marks the advent of pure genre painting in Japanese art, inspired by scenes and special moments of daily life. The subject is absolutely new. It represents a family excursion to Takao, a temple near Kyoto, where the gardens were much admired for their changing autumn colors. The painting depicts a park by a river and an oblique arched bridge that unifies the composition. On the left, we see promenading warrior figures and, on the right, women and children under trees and the ever-present vendor of sweets and drinks. This work foreshadows the realism and simplicity of eighteenth-century prints. At the same time it constitutes the type of subject that pleased customers two centuries before. The artist, Kano Hideyou, second son of Kano Motonobu, created in this work a composite style, adding a personal and incisive touch to the typically decorative accents of his time. This is particularly evident in the faces of his characters and their lively and dynamic attitudes. A contrast is obvious in the treatment of plants, costumes and figures. In the last, a precise function is given to line instead of color, to design instead of painting.

TOSA MITSUYSHI(?). *Moonlight Landscape.* p. 122

The end of the Muromachi period (1337–1573) and the beginning of the following Momoyama period (1586–1615) opened a new act in the pictorial arts of Japan. It was an ephemeral period, lasting not even half a century, but of great importance in the history of the country. The introduction of Christianity in 1549 established the first contacts with Europe. Spanish Mannerist art of the sixteenth century, with its vivid colors and strong tonal contrasts, encountered a perfect echo in the refined and heroic atmosphere of Japan. The so-called military dictators favored the building of grandiose, fortified castles with pompous furnishings in an impressive display of richness and power. Painting was needed to decorate the large walls and pieces of furniture, and elaborate folding screens punctuated the vast spaces. Happily decorative in itself, the *Yamato-e* merged with the *suiboku* technique and met the demands for a large-scale painting. The newly acquired vigor of this technique's large, dazzling brush strokes conferred unexpectedly grandiose and splendid effects.

The new works were named "blue and gold screen" (*konpeki Shohekiga*) for their brilliant colors. The artists depicted birds, flowers and landscape, using greens and blues that stood out against a precious golden background. Kano school artists especially contributed to this genre, as did the Tosa school. It seems we owe to the latter the fusion of *Yamato-e* with *Kara-e,* which is a Chinese style of painting known almost exclusively at the time as *"black and white,"* in the Sung and Yuan traditions. The work illustrated here is attributed to a Tosa artist, Tosa Mitsuyshi (1539–1613). The attribution is uncertain, but indicates the contributions which are credited to that school of artists. They renewed the decorative preciosity of painting and introduced new spatial values and stylization to landscape which they peppered with chromatic accents. Here a river scene is bathed in moonlight. The painting adorns the panels of a screen that originally was a pendant

KANO HIDEYORI
(died 1557)
Excursion to Takao
Middle of the sixteenth century. Muromachi period. Detail. Screen with six panels, painted with colors on paper; 59″ × 145″. Classified among the national treasures.

to a sunny daylight landscape. Gold as a background color alters the whole nocturnal vision which appears vague, uncertain — suggestive more than descriptive. And if the splendor of the golden field should be replaced by the darkness of night, a quarter-moon helps to reveal the mass of pines and willow tree with twisted trunk and branches dripping with gems.

TOSA MITSUYOSHI(?)
Moonlight Landscape
Second half of the sixteenth century.
Muromachi or Momoyama period
Detail of a decoration for a
six-paneled screen; 59 1/4″ by 124 4/5″.

KANO EITOKU(?). *Chao-fu and the Ox.*

This scene was inspired by a typical theme of Chinese art and it is supposed to represent the legendary episode of the Chinese hermits Hsu-yu and Chao-fu who were known for their wisdom. Hsu-yu retired to live alone on a mountain, but the fame of his wisdom spread so that the Emperor invited him to the palace, offering Hsu-yu the throne itself. Hsu-yu not only did not accept, but told the emperor's messenger that the messenger had made him listen to an unclean proposal and for that reason he had to purify his ears

KANO EITOKU(?)
Chai-fu and the Ox
Second half of the sixteenth century.
Momoyama period. Kakemono painted with
ink on paper; 57″ × 20″. The painting is the
second of two scrolls which originally were
to make up the panel decorations of a screen.
Classified among important
national treasures.

in the river's water. He went to the river with his ox and refused to let his oxen drink of the water in which he had washed his ears. Zen artists liked this subject because it scorned worldly activities with exemplary resolve. The painting is attributed to Kano Eitoku (1543–1590), whose incisive light-and-shadow style has left its mark.

KAIHO YUSHO(?). *Allegory of Painting.*

This picture personifies one of the traditional "four arts," which were the harp, chess, calligraphy and painting (*Kin-kisho-ga*). They were an essential part of every noble youth's education and became a favorite subject for artists. Numerous paintings of gentlemen playing chess or the harp have come down to us. Calligraphy and painting, however, were not treated with such reverence, since they were considered as manual arts and gentlemen did not want to have themselves immortalized at work. Thus compositions representing these arts were usually allegorical. Calligraphy was allegorized in the form of a page or a servant preparing ink. Painting was personified by people admiring a painting or an objet d'art. In our illustration, women stare at a landscape of a mountain and flowering tree. Kaiho Yusho (1533–1615), well-known artist of the Momoyana (1586–1615), probably is responsible for the work. He managed to blend the color values of traditional Japanese Yamato painting and the delicate shadings of Chinese art.

KAIHO YUSHO(?)
1533–1615
Allegory of Painting
End of the sixteenth century.
Momoyama period
Detail of a six-panel screen, painted with colors on paper; 61 1/5" × 145 1/2".
Classified among important national treasures.

NO MASK: KO–OMOTE. *Muromachi Period.*

Unlike the *Gigaku* dance masks which often covered the whole head, these can be more properly called masks since they cover only the face. They are neither grotesque nor caricatural. Owing to their abstract characteristics, they were used, as the word *no* indicates (art–representation) for reciting dramas of heros, traditional dances and rites of the primitive Shinto religion. Such dramas had dialogues which were written in verse or prose and were accompanied by dances, choruses, music and chants. Usually the masked protagonist was a woman and represented a divinity, demon or fantastic monstrous beings. The mask was supposed to conjure thoughts of supernatural powers, noble thoughts and fiery passions. Such expressions would be conventionally recognized by the public as personifications of magic ideas, otherworldly force, love, sadness, hate, poverty, madness. In the intermission between dramas were produced short sketches known as *Kyogen,* 125

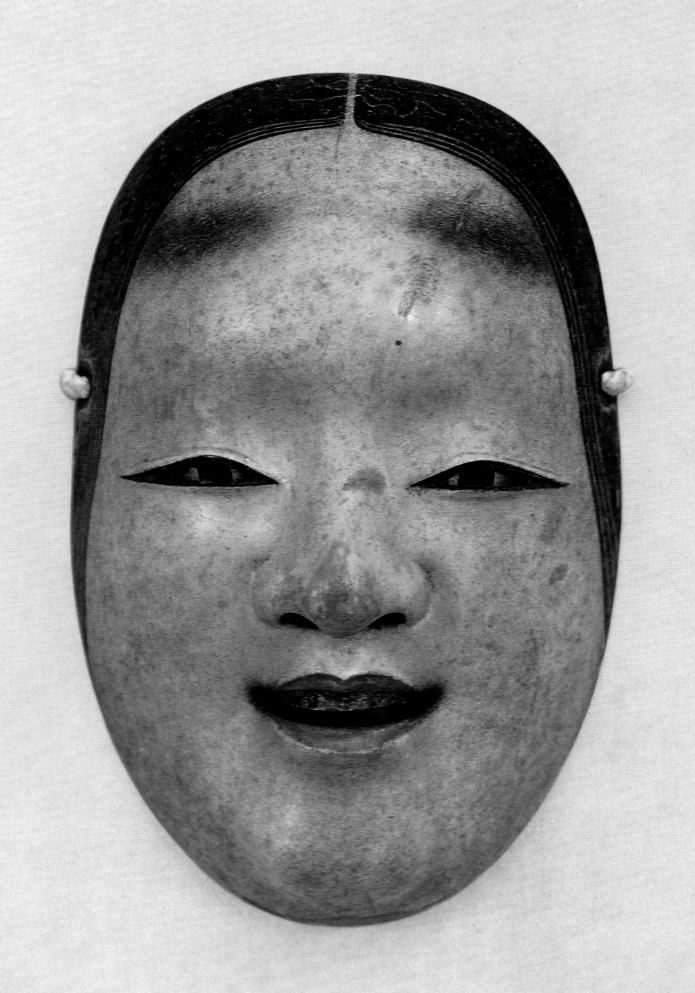

No mask: Ko-omote
First half of the sixteenth century.
Muromachi period
Colored wood;
height 8 1/2″, width 6 1/2″.

or "playful words," in effect farces which also required the use of masks. These were always exaggeratedly comic or fearsome, according to the character of the actor. One of the most beautiful *nō* masks is the *Ko-omote*. It literally means "small face" and has nothing to do with the size of the mask but refers rather to childhood, innocence and freshness. The mask in our illustration reveals these characteristics. The eyes and nose are tenderly childlike, yet the high forehead indicates a precocious intelligence. It may very well be the expression of a young woman dreaming about the innocence of her lost childhood.

DETAIL OF A FABRIC FOR KOSODE. *Momoyama Period.*

The Momoyama period (1586–1615) replaced the wide *kimono* with the *kosode* ("small sleeves"). They were shorter with narrower sleeves and drastically changed the classical form of dress. The design of the *kosode* could be radical, elaborate and sumptuous. This detail illustrates a costume made from material which has been cut in long triangles and sewn so as to alternate a white silk square on a blue blackground and embroidered in lively colors with a splendid design of flowers, pine branches and maple leaves.

Detail of fabric for a kosode
Sixteenth-seventeenth century.
Momoyama period
Silk; height 60 4/5″, shoulders 25 1/2″.

THE BRIDGE OF UJI. *Momoyama or Edo Period.*

As in the moonlit landscape on page 122, this painting treats the theme of the weeping willow and the bridge, a favorite subject of the Momoyama period. But there is a pronounced difference in style between the two works. In the former, the subject is a panorama of night breaking into morning.

The Bridge of Uji
End of the sixteenth–beginning of seventeenth century. Momoyama or Edo period. Screen with six panels painted with colors and gold on paper; 62″ × 127″.

In this work, we see a specific view: the waters of a river which forms eddies around the bridge pylons and causes a water wheel to turn. This painting belongs to a series of "bridges of Uji" which at first were confined to small compositions and were gradually enlarged to fit onto folding screens. Because of the popularity of the subject, the bridge, river and

HASEGAWA TOHAKU
1539–1610
Pine Grove
End of the sixteenth–beginning of the
seventeenth century.
Momoyama period
Panels from a pair of screens of six panels,
painted with ink on paper;
62″ × 138″ each. Classified among
national treasures.

water wheel in Kyoto became famous all over Japan. The work in the illustration is a design that is particularly precise in its lines. Painted in silver, the waves are rather conventionalized, but create a neat transition between the geometric architecture and the shapes of the softer, more luxuriant trees.

HASEGAWA TOHAKU. *Pine Forest.*

This painting of the famous "pine forests of Kyoto," which represents a coppice of trees shrouded in the early morning fog, is among the masterpieces of Hasegawa Tohaku (1539–1610). He was an artist who specialized in landscapes and in compositions of plants and animals. A student in Chinese Sung and Yuan painting (960–1368), Tohaku managed to produce one of the most original adaptations of Chinese ink paintings in Japan. His work illustrates not only the style of Tohaku but also serves as an example of the contribution the Japanese made to the concept of black and white painting. With these reduced means, they were able to create subtle nuances of gray which attained marvelous effects of pure light.

HONAMI KOETSU
AND TAWARAYA SOTATSU
1558–1637
Flowers and Verses
Seventeenth century. Edo period
Kakemono painted in gold and silver
on paper.
Chinese ink calligraphy; 13″ × 27 1/2″.

TAWARAYA SOTATSU AND HONAMI KOETSU. *Flowers and Verses.*

The ephemeral cycle of a lotus which blooms, flowers and dies is captured in this fragment of a gilt-and-silver scroll with poetic verses. The work is the creation of two artists. The painting is attributed to Tawaraya Sotatsu and the writing, conceived in rapid gushing rhythms, is attributed to Honami Koetsu, a versatile artist who figures among the best calligraphers of the period.

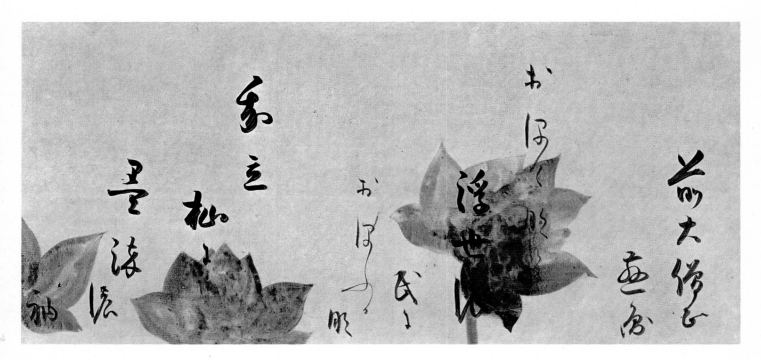

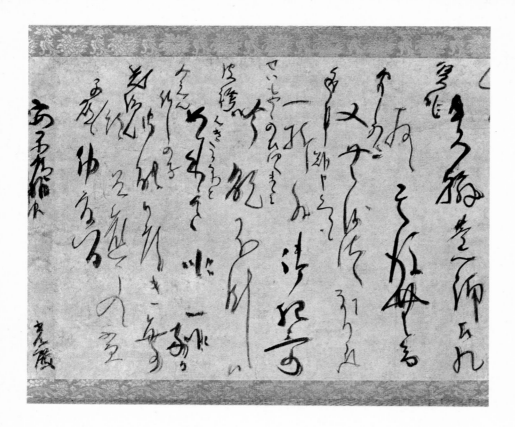

KARASUMARU MITSUHIRO
1579–1638
Text of a letter (1634)
Edo period
Ink calligraphy on paper; 15 1/5″ × 22 1/2″.

KARASUMARU MITSUHIRU.   *Text of a Letter.*

This is the text of a thank-you letter, dated the eighth day of the fifth month of 1634. It is from the poet Karasumaru Mitsuhiru (1579–1638) to the Buddhist monk Aurakuan Sakuden (1554–1642). The latter, a master of the tea ceremony and author of poetry and humorous anecdotes, had sent the former a basket of bamboo shoots and accompanied the present with a short poem by himself, as was the custom at that time.

This writing is considered to be of great beauty for its unadorned elegance and the strength of the brush strokes, revealing the spontaneity and sincerity of the author. He was a noble courtier and a celebrated poet, but, above all, an excellent calligrapher with a rich, sensitive, audaciously modern style.

SCENE OF COUNTRY LIFE.   *Momoyama Period.*

This scene of life on the farm illustrates the annual ceremony of rice transplanting. The women bend over the irrigated field; the men bear on their backs the load of shoots for transplanting; peasants remove mud and sod with their hoes and ox-pulled plows. But the central scene is occupied by the bearers of baskets and containers for food and drinks, and the musicians and masked characters who execute a ritual dance for a good harvest. This is the ceremony of *dengaku,* the "music of the fields," and is a genre scene that adorns, with others, a screen of the Momoyama period (1586–1615). It gives the impression of being definitely removed from decorative painting and any ostentation of gold and colors.

Scene of Country Life
Beginning of the seventeenth century. Momoyama period. Detail of the decoration of a large screen with eight panels painted with colors on a paper; each panel measures 27″ × 16 1/2″.

Scenes of Daily Life in Kyoto
Seventeenth century. Early Edo period
Details of the decoration of a pair of screens
with six panels painted with colors on gilt
paper; each screen 65″ × 136″. Works classified among important national treasures.
Detail: *The Kabuki theater.*

The ancient *Yamato-e* technique re-surfaces here to describe the theme of
a popular, rustic life, a subject which was known from older works.
A renewed love of nature, including the spectacle of rural or city life,
pervades such paintings. With a new figurative vision, they opened the way
for the *ukiyo-e,* the "painting of the floating world," which describes all
that is transient and momentary and yet alive and dynamic in humanity.

SCENES OF POPULAR LIFE IN KYOTO. *First Edo Period.*

The golden background and the genre scenes of these screen paintings ex-
emplify the gradual passage from the decorative Momoyama period to the
more realistic Edo period. Both panels illustrate scenes of city life. To the
right, we see the Kyoto Bridge on the river Kamo, a boatman mooring on
the banks, some buildings, a barber shop with its sign representing the
utensils of the trade and a customer being shaved. A rider and his retinue,
flanked by peddlers in the street, are getting ready to cross the bridge. In
the painting above, we see, in the center scene, a kabuki theater with the
musicians on stage and the audience seated in the pit, fragments of the
bridge and figures of men and women fording the river. Such works nar-
rate the city life. We are on the threshold of *ukiyo-e,* a style which captured the various aspects of daily existence and tried to illustrate the new

Scenes of Daily Life in Kyoto
Detail: *The Bridge of Kyoto on the Kamo
River*

fashions and costumes characterizing people in the big cities. It showed detailed ceremonial scenes, parties, games and work, landscapes and still-lifes. It depicted family scenes or adventurous episodes from literature and the theater. It represented anonymous crowds, groups of men and women, common and illustrious personages. Above all, it treated the portraits of actors and courtesans, famous fancy women, prostitutes from the pleasure-quarter. A modern and unprejudiced spirit prevailed, representing with power, precision and penetration the new world that fermented within the traditional institutions. This provided an inexhaustible repertory for a group of works that still remain as the authentic expression of a restless humanity. There was vast production of paintings and wood-cuts, in black and white and in color, in an exuberant and often vigorous style.

Although this was the first realistic subject matter in Japanese art, its style and form never denied the traditions from which the school was matured and derived. And even if it refuted the religious, profane and secular repertories of Chinese inspiration, it did not free itself from the imperatives of traditional art. The realism of the subjects and their vivacity broke down the pedantic attitudes of painters of the old school. Many painters, however, still followed traditional esthetic canons. And the influence of tradition is evident in the development of the new, naturalistic elements.

HISHIKAWA MORONOBU(?)
The "Kabuki"
Seventeenth century. Edo period
Painted with colors on paper.
Detail of the decoration of a pair
of screens; each 68" × 154 4/5".

HISHIKAWA MORONOBU(?). *The Kabuki.*
This painting depicts the preparations for a *kabuki* play. The actors are wearing their costumes and the musicians are tuning their instruments. On the basis of style, this work is attributed to Hishikawa Moronobu (1619–1695), considered to be the founder of *ukiyo-e,* and noted not only for his paintings but also for his famous Yoshiwara black and white prints. Some of them were colored by hand and they reproduced scenes and characters from the well-known pleasure-quarter in the capital. Moronobu forcefully introduced the kabuki into the figurative repertory of *ukiyo-e* and it remained one of the favorite subjects of Japanese print-makers. Kabuki is a popular form of Japanese theater that lent itself well to express the ideals and tastes of the middle-classes. Its origins date back to 1600. A young dancer from the Izumo shinto sanctuary, named O-Kuni, organized a program during the holidays. The representations were a success

137

and this marked the beginning of a popular show that was later set to music and adapted to different central themes. Scrolls and screens show us what the theaters and plays in the first decades of the seventeenth century looked like.

Dish decorated with flowers and birds
Second half of the seventeenth century.
Edo period
Detail. Porcelain of the "ancient Kutani" type; height 3 1/2", diameter 17".
Classified among important national treasures.

NONOMURA NINSEI. *Vase with Prunus Flowers.*

A light enamel covers the entire surface of this vase (below), except the lower part that shows the natural color of terra cotta and indicates to the viewer that this is not a porcelain piece. The decoration is an exuberant composition of prunus flowers and branches among golden clouds. The vase is classified among the *ommoyaki,* a type of precious pottery which is enameled in white or ivory. The most famous painters of the Kano and Tosa schools collaborated with Japanese potters in the application of polychrome naturalistic designs. The vase illustrated is by Nonomura Ninsei, a noted Kyoto potter active toward the middle of the seventeenth century. He learned his art in the school of a Korean master and manufactured pottery in the form of tea sets, decanters, boxes and bird-shaped incense burners. He made extensive use of low-temperature glazes, treating them with the delicacy of a painter. He composed landscapes, geometrical designs and flowers and buds in a vivid gamut of opaque colors, and often imitated the lacquer technique, interpreting his motifs in low-relief with an astonishing virtuosity.

NONOMURA NINSEI
Vase with prunus flowers
Second half of the seventeenth century.
Edo period
Glazed earthware; height 12".
Classified among important
national treasures.

FROM A DISH DECORATED WITH BIRDS AND FLOWERS. *Edo Period.*

The decorative perfection achieved by Japanese porcelain is exemplified in this composition of birds and flowers adorning a large "ancient Kutani" dish of the second half of the seventeenth century. The style resembles that of Chinese porcelains of the Ch'ing period (1644–1912) and particularly those of the Kang-hsi period (1662–1722). The design and color of this piece are typically Japanese, even if it dates from the first period in the history of porcelain in Japan. It seems that the manufacture of porcelain was introduced into Japan in the sixteenth century by Korean potters who settled in the Kyushu island. Only in 1616 was "China clay" discovered in Izumuyama and this allowed the manufacture of porcelain on a large scale. A great number of Korean potters then moved to Sarayama, in the Arita region, to be close to the source of clay. There they founded an industry that has flourished until present. Toward the second half of the seventeenth century the feudal lord Toshiharu Maeda ordered the potter Sayuo Goto to build some kilns in the village of Kutani. The potters there followed the production of Arita, identifying their products with a deeper and more intense chromatic gamut. They used dark yellow, red, blue and green, applied with a vigorous brush onto flowers, birds, landscapes and geometrical designs. The dish shown here dates from the early period of Kutani porcelain.

Dish decorated with fences and vine shoots
Beginning of the eighteenth century.
Edo period
Detail of the decoration.
Nabeshima porcelain; diameter 12".

DISH DECORATED WITH FENCES AND VINE SHOOTS. *Edo Period.*
This composition with vine shoots over two fences reveals the extent to
which Japanese potters used color with exquisite pictorial taste. The background for the design is the opalescent white of the dish material itself as
well as the shaded blue of the reed fences. The red, yellow and green leaves
stand out on them, as do the red tendrils designed in soft calligraphic
lines. The decoration is typical of Nabeshima ceramics, manufactured in
the workshops of the Nabeshima family in the Saga province. The manufacture was started in Okawachi at the beginning of the eighteenth century, and the dish shown dates from their first period. Nabeshima artists
employed a wide repertory of subjects, including birds, fruits, flowers and
landscape elements, such as bridges, brooks and fences. The shaded tonalities were obtained with techniques similar to those used in dyeing clothes.

ATSUITA TYPE COSTUME FOR THE NO THEATER. *Edo Period.*
The type of *kimono* or *kosode* known as *atsuita* indicates a robe used by
no theater actors interpreting male characters. The materials are usually
simple and the ornamentation austere and sober. The example shown is

Atsuita type costume for the No theater
First half of the seventeenth century.
Edo period
Silk; height 57", shoulders 26 1/2".

HONAMI KOETSU
Writing box
Beginning of the seventeenth century.
Edo period
Lacquered wood;
height 4 1/2''; length 9 1/2'', width 9''.
Classified among important
national treasures.

OGATA KORIN
1658–1716 *Writing box*
Second half of the seventeenth century.
Edo period. Lacquered wood;
height 55 1/2'', length 11'', width 7 4/5''.
Classified among important
national treasures.

OGATA KORIN
The God of Wind and Thunder
Beginning of the eighteenth century.
Edo period. Pair of screens with two panels,
painted with colors and gold background
on paper, 66 1/2'' × 73'' each.
Classified among the important
national treasures.

an exception for its luxuriousness, but corresponds to the prevailing taste of the Momoyama period (1586–1615) and the early Edo period (1615–1867). The costume is made in two pieces, one in gold cloth and the other in red silk. The calligraphic decoration in gold on red and violet softens the blending of the colors. The ideograms and the syllabic signs (*hiragana*), painted in elegant free hand, are assymetrically spaced to emphasize the different verses of the short poems about spring. The unknown decorator chose these from the Wakan Roei-shu, an anthology of Chinese and Japanese poems compiled about 1000 A.D.

HONAMI KOETSU. *Writing Box.*

The golden age of Japanese lacquer was the brief but splendid Momoyama period (1573–1615), when all crafts achieved an elegance and distinction still unsurpassed. This writing set is by Honami Koetsu (1558–1637), a painter who lived in both the Momoyama and Edo (1615–1867) periods and who also decorated ceramics and lacquer ware. For the latter, he used the ancient technique of *ashide*. But opposed to *ashide's* basically cryptographic form, Koetsu's writing is transparent, ornamental and of a high literary value.

The decoration on this box transcribes a brief poem by Minamoto no Hitoshi (880–951), contained in the *Gosen Waka-shu,* an anthology compiled in 951 A.D. The subject is the Sano boat bridge in the eastern provinces and the decoration is composed of a row of boats in dull gold, diagonally crossed by a fine lead plate representing the flooring of the bridge. The beautiful italic characters transcribing the poem are in silver relief, except the words "boat bridge" which are suggested, riddle-like, by the design. The poem says: "The boat bridge in Sano, in the east, reminds me of the love that embraces the void between us; but, alas, she does not know how much I love her!"

OGATA KORIN. *Writing Box.*

As a departure from most desk sets, this box has two compartments, the lower one to keep a stock of paper scrolls. The decorations by the famous painter Ogata Korin (1685–1716), one of the greatest artists of the Edo period (1615–1867), is in *maki-e* on a black lacquer background with mother-of-pearl encrustations and metal inlays. The design is inspired from a scene of the *Ise Monogatari,* the classical "Ise tales," and reproduces a small bridge in lead plate in a garden of golden iris and mother-of-pearl flowers.

OGATA KORIN. *The God of Wind and Thunder.*

The subject of the god of wind and thunder unleashing the elements had already been treated before Korin by Tawaraya Sotatsu (1576–1643). Sotatsu, together with Honami Koetsu (1558–1637), had firmly established the Japanese tradition of artist-decorators. Two generations later, Ogata Korin, son of a wall-paper painter and grand-nephew of Sotatsu, picked up all the subjects of the great masters, enriching them with dazzling colors and exuberant design. His style had humor and a sense of

caricature, and although it perpetuated the decorative tendency of the Momoyama period, his chromatic technique surpassed even Sotatsu. The latter, in a painting on the same subject adorning a pair of Kenminji screens in Kyoto, had previously drawn some black clouds on a gold background — a new way of using ink. Korin also used the device to give greater depth to his figures. But he went even further in the use of ink, mixing it to other colors and obtaining dark grays and greens that he used instead of black to draw the outlines of the designs.

KAIGETSUDO ANDO
1672–1743
Woman in the Wind
Eighteenth century.
Edo period
Kakemono painted with colors on silk;
38″ × 17″.

144

KAIGETSUDO ANDO.   *Woman in the Wind.*
Kaigetsudo Ando, active in Edo between 1688 and 1715 (and exiled afterwards because of a scandal), immortalized in *ukizu-e* the ideal portrait of a prosperous matron dressed in luxurious brocades. The illustration is supposed to portray a courtesan from Yoshiwara, the pleasure-district of the capital. The seal on the work reads "Japanese painting done for fun." The author was proud of his style which in its time was considered to be bizarre and non-conformist, destined to undermine the classical esthetic canons of the Kano and Tosa schools.

SUZUKI HARUNOBU
1725–1770
O-sen of Kasamori (circa 1769)
Edo period
Woodcut on paper (*nishiki-e*);
11″ × 7 1/2″.

SUZUKI HARUNOBU.   *Beautiful O-Sen from Kasamori.*
O-Sen, from the tea-house of the Tuani sanctuary in Kasamori, was reputed to be one of the most beautiful women in the city of Edo. Suzuki Harunobu (1725–1770) portrayed her seated on a porch in conversation with a fan-peddler. The portrait made both Harunobu and O-sen famous throughout Japan. Harunobu dominated the art of *ukuyo-e* during the middle of the eighteenth century. He is recognized traditionally as the inventor of full color printing, a technique known as *nishiki-e,* or "brocade painting," that the artist also used to illustrate books and calendars.

His delicate personal style is evident in the calm, harmonious colors, in the linear planes and in the fluid play of the lines in the robes of the two characters. The designs in the fans are of actors and coats-of-arms, autographed by noted painters of the time.

IKE NO TAIGA. *Landscapes with Pavilions.*

During the eighteenth century, "intellectual painting" (*bunjinga*), a movement by poet-painters and intellectual-painters, took a wide hold in Japan. The artists identified themselves with a corresponding tendency in Chinese art and advocated a return to spiritual, artistic values, opposing decorative formalism and realistic rendering. Ike no Taiga (1728–1776), together with Yosa no Buson (1716–1783), was one of the greatest exponents of this tendency, ultimately derived from Southern Sung Chinese art (1127–1280). It underwent further development in Japan and created the *haiga,* a combination of painting and poetry that considerably influenced calligraphic art. The landscapes illustrated above are classic *bunjinga* works and the Chinese influence should be noticed not only in the style of the composition as a whole, but also in the vision of the vastness of nature and of man who becomes a mere landscape element. The first illustration shows the park around the Shuai-weng pavilion. A literary

IKE NO TAIGA
1723–1776
Landscape with Pavilions
Detail: *Shuai-weng pavilion of Hsu-chou.*
Second half of the eighteenth century. Edo period. Details of the decoration in a pair of screens with six panels. Painted with colors and gold background on paper; 67 1/2″ × 149″ each. Classified among national treasures.

146

Detail: *Boat mooring on the banks of the Hsi-hu, the lake west of Hang-chou.*

meeting is gathered in the large room opening on the porch; the people are guests of Ou Yang-hsin, Governor of Hsu-chou. The second illustration shows a boat moving near the banks of Lake Hsi-hu, in Hang-chou, capital of southern Sung. Ike no Taiga renews the favorite subject of the early Kano school artists. The following illustration, on page 148, shows the Yo-yang-lou pavilions on the fortified lake banks. The subject was inspired by a literary meeting that took place there at the beginning of the eighth century under the hospitality of Governor Hang-chou.

The subject of these "landscapes with pavilions" celebrates the ancient Chinese custom of holding literary meetings. These poetic tournaments were periodically patronized by the higher magistrates. Although the environment is in classical Chinese taste, the composition is almost amateurishly informal, and the trees have been treated with an almost pointillist or dotting technique.

147

IKE NO TAIGA
Landscapes with pavilions
Detail: *The pavilion of Yo-yang-lou on the
banks of the lake west of Hang-chou.*

KATSUKAWA SHUNSHO. *Portrait of the Actor Sawamura Sojuro.*

Sawamura Sojuro (1689–1756) was a famous actor of the Edo period (1615–1867) and the head of a long dynasty of *kabuki* players. The main feature of this portrait is that the actor is seen off-stage, portrayed in his dressing room with Yamashita Mankiku, another famous actor who specialized in female roles and is shown here fully dressed as a lady. This was an innovation of painter and engraver Katsukawa Shunsho (1729–1792) who departed from the conventional *ukiyo-e* subject of depicting

KATSUKAWA SHUNSHO
1729–1792
Portrait of the Actor Sawamura Sojuro
(circa 1781)
Edo period
Woodcut on paper (*nishiki-e*);
14 1/2″ ×10″.

TORII KIYONAGA
1752–1815
The Geisha Tachibana (circa 1781)
Edo period
Woodcut on paper (*nishiki-e*);
15 1/2″ × 10 1/2″.

actors in their famous roles. He showed them at different times in their activities, getting ready for the stage or returning to their dressing-rooms after the show. This intimate atmosphere within a precise decorative frame gave new life to the *ukiyo-e* style of actors' portraiture.

TOSHUSAI SHARAKU
Portrait of an Actor
Edo period
Printed on paper; 12 1/2″ × 5 1/2″

TOSHUSAI SHARAKU. *Portrait of an Actor*.

This full-figure portrait shows actor Otani Oniji II in the role of Kawashima Jirogoro, a truculent dramatic character. It was part of a series of prints in *nishiki-e* for the summer kabuki season of 1794. The expressiveness of this portrait is characteristic of its author. Toshusai Sharaku of the *ukiyo-e* school was prominent among Japanese woodcut artists. His portraits of *no* and kabuki actors are rigorous and penetrating works of great power and originality. From May, 1794, to February, 1795, Sharaku made 145 prints, but little is known of him before and after this period. Tradition has it that, after being in the service of feudal lord Hachisuka, he became an actor in the *no* theater. He started print-making in 1790, specializing in portraits of actors. He is pointed to as the inventor of *kirara-e* or *unmozuri,* a form of engraving on mica plates. Some works printed in that technique are dated 1794.

TORII KIYONAGA. *Geisha Tachibana.*

This print is from the series "a collection of beauties from the pleasure-district" and shows a famous geisha getting ready to enter the room to join her guests. Preceded by an escort, she turns toward the friend seated behind her, who is putting the finishing touches to her make-up.

Torii Kiyonaga, an *ukiyo-e* artist of the fourth Torii generation, followed the family tradition of actors' portraiture. In a second period, he started his studies of "young beauties" in which he excelled with his soft and lively style. His compositions are famous for the delicacy of the lines resulting from his superb woodcut technique. The "beauty in the Kiyonaga style" became one of the best examples of the Japanese ideal of feminine beauty. The print illustrated is dated 1781 and belongs to the early period of his portraits of women.

KITAGAWA UTAMARO. *Female Portrait.* p. 152

This figure portrays a young beauty in a "coquettish attitude." She is part of a series of "ten studies of female expressions" by Kitagawa Utamaro (1754–1806), one of the major exponents of *ukiyo-e* art and a master of female portraits. At first he devoted his talents to portraits of actors and then of young courtesans in the manner of Torii Kiyonaga (1752–1815).

KITAGAWA UTAMARO
1754–1806
Portrait of a Woman (circa 1791)
Edo Period
Woodcut on paper; 15″ × 9 1/2″.

He began in 1790 to form a very personal style, executing a series of works known as *okubi-e*, sketch-like images with busts and faces in the foreground, framed by complicated coiffures. The print illustrated here is a *okubi-e* and is characteristic of a figurative conception which soberly expresses the model's features, emphasizing expression, character and the minute particulars of pose and costume. We see here a young woman whose hands pull at an edge of her dress, as if enjoying the sensual contact with the fabric, a precious brocade with birds in flight. Her elaborate hair-do contrasts with the simple linearity of her face and the soft line of her shoulder and partially exposed breast.

AOKI MOKUBEI. *Daybreak on the Uji.*

A very personal style marks this landscape in which the fresh morning atmosphere is colored by the first rays of the sun. The specificity of the place, the river Uji, indicates an actual panorama, but the artist has turned this lovely site into an ideal vision. Aoki Mokubei (1767–1833) was a famous potter as well as a noted painter. He managed to breathe space and volume into his paintings and an impressionistic sensibility which he inherited from the *bunjinga* masters.

AOKI MOKUBEI
1767–1833
Daybreak on the Uji (1824)
Edo period
Kakemono painted with colors on paper
19 1/2″ × 23 1/2″.
Classified among important
national treasures.

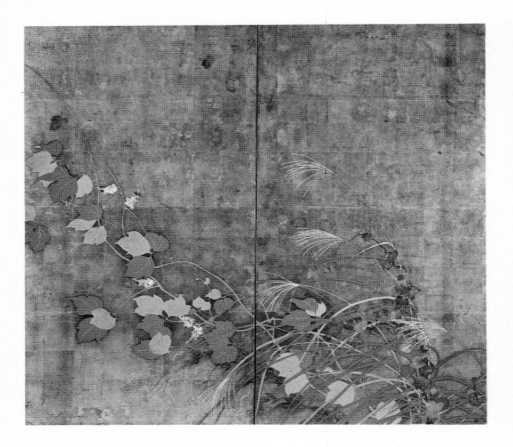

SAKAI HOITSU. *Autumn Wind and Summer Rain.*

These works are among the last masterpieces of decorative Japanese painting. It has been suggested that Sakai Hoitsu, the great disciple of the school of Sotatsu and Korin who was still active in the early years of the nineteenth century, got his idea for this pair of screens from compositions of the divinities of wind and thunder. Instead of using personifications of his subjects, he preferred to show their effects on nature. The invisible wind has bent over the autumn plants and detached the yellow leaves from their branches. A shower has poured upon the summer vegetation and we see that a rivulet has formed.

The typical conventionalism of decorator artists is manifested in the metallic tint in the background. In these works, the artist used a silver background and silver and blue for the water. But the rest of the composition is based on naturalistic colors and details.

SAKAI HOITSU
1761–1828
Autumn Wind and Summer Rain
Beginning of the nineteenth century.
Edo period
Pair of screens with two panels.
Painted on paper; 66″ × 73″ each.
Classified among important
natural treasures.
Above: *Autumn Wind.*
154 Right: *Summer Rain.*

155

KATSUSHIKA HOKUSAI. *Hodogaya.*
In this work we see on a tree-lined street some travelers who have stopped
in front of a breathtaking view of Mount Fuji. This is among the last pure
Japanese landscape attempts before the definitive encounter with Western

KATSUSHIKA HOKUSAI
1760–1849
Hodogaya (1823–1831)
Edo period
From the series "The Thirty-six Views of
Mount Fuji."
Woodcut on paper (*nishiki-e*): 10″ × 15″.

art. In such an interpretation, man and nature seem to be perfectly reconciled. Man is no longer born an element of nature nor a protagonist of it, but simply another anecdotal subject. The little bearer with an emaciated nude chest energetically mops the sweat from his head while his companion ties his shoelaces. A sense of oppression and fatigue permeates the travelers. The work is taken from the "Thirty-six Views of Mount Fuji" by Katsushika Hokusai, a group of colored wood prints that the artist did as a follow-up to his "One Hundred Views of Fuji" of 1817. They reveal his inventiveness, the rich originality in the various views of the mountain, which is seen from every possible direction. All the compositions betray the strangeness of their author, one of the most complex personalities in the history of Japanese art. In addition to his exceptional talent, Hokusai was indefatigable. At 65, he called himself an "old man gone mad for drawing." He was an eclectic artist who assimilated every style and technique in traditional Japanese painting as well as in Chinese and European art and painted every subject that was offered to him. He illustrated stories and dramas, decorated scrolls and screens, composed an incalculable number of prints — more than 30,000 have been attributed to him. Countless stories about his bizarre life have been handed down, like his wanting at all costs to paint a horse on a piece of paper 210 yards square. Given his prolific nature, his work is certainly unequal, depending as he did on the inspiration of the moment. But his profound understanding of his tradition gave a magnificent coda to the arts of Japan.

WATANABE KAZAN. *Portrait of Takami Senseki.*   *p. 158*
The samurai of Osaka, who had distinguished himself by putting down the revolt of Oshio, Takami Senseki was a friend and patron of Watanabe Kazan and urged him to study art. In this portrait, an extremely realistic rendering of a noble face, Watanabe Kazan reveals his style in all its originality, a combination of Western realism and Oriental idealism. One of the most developed sensibilities in Japan in the Edo period (1615–1867), Kazan foreshadowed the modernization of his country and prophesied a politics of isolation in order to bring about a stable and peaceful coexistence with the rest of the world. Kazan was an admirer of European art, especially of the Dutch school, which, for some reason, was best known in Japan. He liked the realism of the Lowland masters and their way of modeling with light and shade.   **157**

WATANABE KAZAN
1793–1841
Portrait of Takami Senseki (1837)
Edo period
Kakemono painted with colors on silk;
46″ × 23″.
Classified among the national treasures.

ANDO HIROSHIGE
1797–1858
View of Shono (1833)
Edo period
Xylography on paper (*nishiki-e*);
10 4/5″ × 15 4/5″.

ANDO HIROSHIGE. *View of Shono.*

It has been justifiably observed that in the landscapes of Hiroshige the viewer gets soaked with the rain, his feet sink into the snow and he gets warmed by the sun. The impression of driving rain is overwhelming in this woodcut which shows us a glimpse of the Shono landscape, one of the "Fifty-three Stations of Tokaido," part of the famous "Way of the Eastern Sea." Ando Hiroshige (1797–1858) dedicated a series of prints to this beautiful panorama. A few travelers are hurrying to village houses in the valley, others are climbing up the hill, protecting themselves with their wide straw hats. The simplicity of the composition, together with its beauty of color, evokes rather than reproduces a landscape. Through an attentive observation of nature, Hiroshige succeeded in creating in his works a luminous and dreamy atmosphere drenched with sentiment and lyricism.

UEMURA SHOEN. *Flames (The Rokujo Woman).* *p. 160*

In her beautiful costume, adorned with flowers and spider webs, Rokujo, a character from *Genji Mongatari,* the immortal eleventh-century "novel of the shining prince," is tormented amidst the "flames" of jealousy. Her body slightly bent, her ear cocked, she seems to be listening; her face takes on the impenetrable look of a wax mask.

Uemura Shoen's work reveals the classicizing effort in Japanese modern art. She was one of the most sensitive Japanese women portraitists and knew how to penetrate the psychological spirit of her figures, which she took from both traditional iconography and daily life.

On page 160:
UEMURA SHOEN
1875–1949
Flames (1918)
(The Rokujo Woman)
Taisho era
Kakemono painted with colors on silk;
75 1/2″ × 36″.

159

HISTORY OF THE MUSEUMS
AND THEIR BUILDINGS

HISTORY OF THE COLLECTIONS

Today's Tokyo National Museum bears no resemblance to the original one which was cut out of rock in the Temple of Yushima Seido in Tokyo. This volume was created for the purpose of presenting the museum's sculptures, ceramics, objects, paintings, and calligraphies and so a history of the museum which preserves and exhibits these art works seems appropriate.

Since antiquity, the Japanese have loved and respected historical and artistic rarities. The first museum, the Shosoin, was built for the preservation of the treasures of the Nara period and the Shogun of the Murmachi period promoted its exhibitions and collections. In these old institutions we find a few of the characteristics which we attribute today to museums, but it was the Meiji period which first exhibited artistic and historical objects for the purpose of educating a large audience. A new museum with this aim, the Museum of Yushima, was instituted in 1871.

At that time, the Japanese began to build museums for social and educational reasons as well as to preserve Japanese culture. Two scholars, Machida Hisanari and Tanaka Yoshio, went during the Meiji restoration to the Occident to take a look at the Western world's museums, and when they returned they made it known to the government that Japan needed such institutions for educating its public and developing its culture. Intellectuals were embittered to see how art of the past had been destroyed by violent social changes during the Meiji restoration and by neglect owing to the new fashion for Western art. In 1871 the government issued a decree called the "Preservation of Ancient Objects" which required registration of all antiquities and works of art.

The material collected by the Museum of Yushima was, at first, vast and mixed. In addition to artistic and historical objects, there were scientific and natural-history exhibits. But soon the available space became cramped and the museum was transferred to the former residence of the Shimazu a Koji-machi family in whose restored and enlarged buildings exhibition halls were set up. This arrangement lasted from 1873 to 1882.

The collection was enlarged in various ways. International exhibitions played a very important role. Objects of all types were brought together for the International Exposition of Vienna in 1873 and some of these, in addition to foreign works that were bought abroad, ended up in the museum halls. The same thing happened at the 1878 Paris Exposition, when a number of objects of even greater value were deposited in the museum. One of these is the famous lacquered writing box of Ogata Korin (p. 142). Naturally, the Japanese did not only depend on exhibition material and during this time made marked efforts to acquire works. The Heian period painting, *Fugen Bosatsu* (pp. 86–87), Honami Koetsu's lacquered writing box (p. 142), Nonomura Ninsei's vase with prunus flowers and other masterpieces were acquired in 1878. Only 50 yen (about ten cents) was paid for the *Fugen Bosatsu,* which at the time was considered expensive.

In 1882 the museum was moved from Kojimachi to its present site in the Ueno public garden. The Second National Exposition Art Pavilion was used as a building. Designed by the English architect J. Condle, the building had two floors and for a long time was one of the most popular spots in the Ueno Park.

In 1887 the museum entered a new phase of development. More attention was paid to the study of humanities and less attention to using the museum as a building for international expositions. Before, the museum had been under the jurisdiction of the Ministry of Agriculture and Commerce; in 1886, it was assigned to the Ministry of the Imperial Palace and renamed the Imperial Palace Museum. In 1895, the Museum of Nara was inaugurated and in 1897, the Museum of Kyoto was opened. In 1908 the Kokeikan Art Gallery (Palace of Congratulations) was completed. A neo-Baroque building, it was dedicated in honor of the crown prince's wedding.

In 1923 the main building, dating from 1881, was badly damaged by the earthquake which devastated the Kanto provinces. It was decided in 1928 that the museum's main building should be made over as a gift to the Imperial Palace and, as such, would be devoted to ancient Japanese art. Thus the museum took on a new character and became the only museum set aside for art alone. The present building is Oriental in style. The construction funds were gathered from public subscription; completed in 1937, the building was opened in 1939.

When the main building was under reconstruction, the gardens were also done over and two buildings, the Okyo-kan and the Kujo-kan, were put up in the back garden. The former was originally the writing room of Myoganin, a temple in Aichi. A precious architectural jewel constructed in 1742, the edifice was given to the Ministry of Tkashi Masuda. On the walls are paintings by Okyo Maruyama. Kujo-kan was given in 1934 by Michihide Kujo and was originally part of the Kujo family villa in Tokyo. Landscapes with pagodas figure on its sliding doors and walls.

In order to protect the Museum during World War II, the exhibits were moved to the Kyoto provinces, but, after the War, they were brought back to Tokyo and the museum reopened in March, 1946.

In 1947, when the new Constitution placed the Museum under the direction of the Ministry of Public Instruction, it was named the National Museum and, in 1950, became the Tokyo National Museum. The major events which have affected the museum since have been the construction of Horyuji-kan in 1954 for the treasures given by the Imperial Palace in 1887, and the foundation of the Oriental Museum which should be finished by the end of 1968.

Eleven thousand paintings, more than 2,700 calligraphies, and 1,600 sculptures, 33,400 craft objects and 37,000 archeological pieces — totaling 86,000 objects — make up the Museum's holdings. Through purchases, private donations and the incorporation of collections from earlier museums, the inventory has expanded enormously.

By means of exchanges with other countries, major stone sculptures have been acquired, and paintings and stuccos as well as Etruscan works have been added to the collection of a Museum that now must be considered as one of the most important in the world.

Jô Okada

THE DEPARTMENTS

The Museum's patrimony is grouped into the following departments: archeology, decorative arts (fabrics, metals, weapons, ceramics, lacquer ware) and the fine arts (sculpture, paintings, calligraphy).

Archeology — This department owns more than 36,000 pieces, mainly from the Period of the Mounds as well as from the Jomon and Yayoi periods. There are also objects from Korea, China, Europe and the Americas, making for a total of more than 50,000 pieces. Also included is ethnographic material from the Japanese islands, from Formosa, Korea and the Pacific archipelagos.

Fabrics — Two major collections, numbering approximately 3,500 examples, are in this department. Both Japanese and Chinese, the works include private and ceremonial clothes and their accessories, decorative materials and dolls.

Metals — 20,000 coins, utensils, temple ornaments, furniture, bronze mirrors, etc., make up this department.

Weapons — Mostly swords, which are divided into three categories called *Ko-to, Shin-to* and *Shin-shin-to,* make up this department.

Ceramics — There are about 5,000 pieces among the ceramics, porcelains and glass in this department.

Lacquer Ware — Metal and mother-of-pearl inlays, *maki-e* (lacquer of gold), paintings on lacquer, carved lacquer, ivories, and worked bamboo are part of the department's 5,000 pieces. Chinese, Japanese and Korean, they include musical instruments, furniture, games, religious tea-ceremony objects, burners, architectural models, ship models, carriages, cosmetic boxes, various writing articles.

Sculpture — Although the nucleus of this department's 5,000 pieces centers on Japanese sculpture from the Asuka, Nara, Muromachi and Kamakura periods, there are also sculptures from Grandhara (Pakistan), Hudda (Afghanistan) and Yun-kang (China). They are mostly Buddhist works. There are also theater masks and modern sculptures.

Pictures — This department houses nearly 12,500 works (paintings, prints, drawings, monumental reliefs). Various schools, from ancient times to the present, are included.

Calligraphy — Preserving close to 2,500 examples of calligraphic writing, this department has a balance between Japanese and Chinese works: sutra manuscripts (Buddhist texts) from the Nara period, prose and poetry compositions in Chinese characters (*kanji*), Japanese syllabaries (*kana*), writings on decorated paper and autographs of historical figures.

Exhibitions — Over an eight-mile area, 30,000 objects can be displayed. The guiding concept in exhibiting them is to furnish a thorough art and cultural history of Japan and other countries.

In the Horyuji Jomotsuka building there is a treasure made up of 300 pieces which originally belonged to the Nara temple of the same name. It was presented to the Emperor in 1878.

THE BUILDING

The Tokyo National Museum is a complex of structures set among the trees and lawns of a park. There are three principal buildings: The Museum itself was constructed after the 1923 earthquake in a modern, monumental style in commemoration of the coronation of the emperor; it includes 20 halls for exhibitions. The Hokeikan, another building, dating from 1908, was built in the style of the 1900 Paris Exposition; it commemorates the wedding of the crown prince; it has eight exhibition halls. The most recent section is a gallery containing the Horyuji treasures, called Horyuji Homotsukan. There are also outbuildings (lecture halls, library, restaurant) and a few historical buildings in the area of the park, like the Okyo-kan, the Edo period residential house and the Tengo-an, the Shunso-ro tea house and the Rokuso-an.

The museum's patrimony is relatively recent. An early gallery was set up by the government in 1871 at Seido, Kanda, Tokyo; ten years later, the Ueno park museum was constructed under imperial jurisdiction. In 1947 the Museum of the Imperial Palace was put under the direction of the Minister of Education and became a national museum.

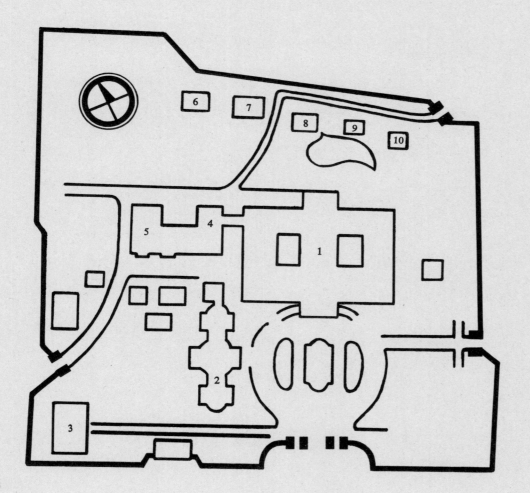

DIAGRAM

MAIN BUILDING	1
HOKEIKAN	2
HORYUJI TREASURES GALLERY (Horyuji Homotsukan)	3
OFFICES	4
AUDITORIUM	5
KUJI-KAN	6
OKYO-KAN	7
ROKUSO-AN	8
TENGO-AN	9
SHUNSO-RO	10

The museum plans have been reproduced by permission of the Tokyo National Museum.

MAIN FLOOR

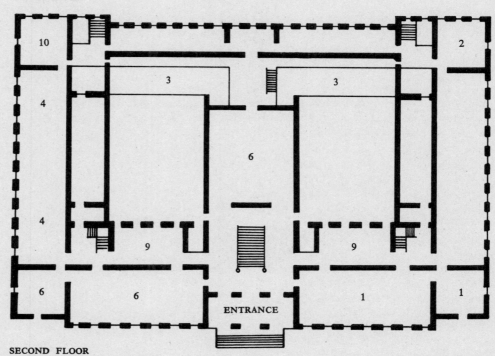

MAIN BUILDING

ARCHEOLOGY	1
FABRICS	2
METALS	3
CERAMICS	4
LACQUER WARE	5
SCULPTURE	6
PAINTING	7
CALLIGRAPHY	8
EXHIBITIONS	9
WEAPONS	10
GRAPHICS	11

ENTRANCE

SECOND FLOOR

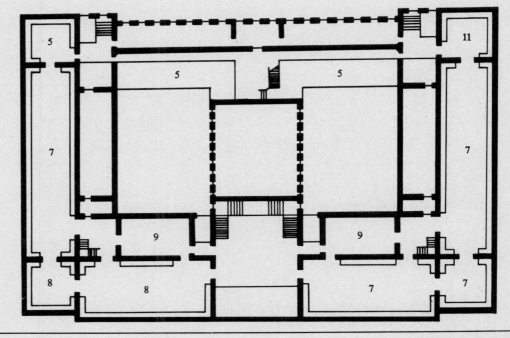

HOKEIKAN

JOMON PERIOD	1
YAYOI PERIOD	2
KOFUN PERIOD	3
EXCAVATION OBJECTS	4
EXHIBITIONS	5

MAIN FLOOR   SECOND FLOOR

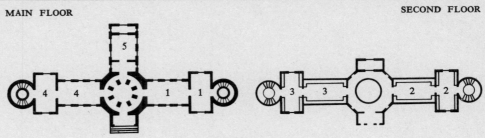

BASIC BIBLIOGRAPHY

MUSEUM WORKS

JAPANESE NATIONAL COMMISSION FOR UNESCO, Museums in Japan. Tokyo, 1960.
NATIONAL COMMISSION FOR PROTECTION OF CULTURAL PROPERTIES, Administration for Protection of Cultural Properties in Japan. Tokyo, 1962.

GUIDEBOOKS

L. P. ROBERTS, The Connoisseur's Guide to Japanese Museums. Tokyo, 1967.

CATALOGUES

Tokyo Kokuritsu Hakubutsukan Shuzohin Mokuroku, 3 vols. Tokyo, 1957.
(Catalogue of the Tokyo National Museum Collections)
Tokyo Kokuritsu Hakubutsukan Meihin Hyakusen (100 Masterpieces of the Tokyo National Museum). Tokyo, 1959.
Tokyo Kokuritsu Hakubutsukan (The Tokyo National Museum), 3 vols. Tokyo, 1966.
The works and collections of the Tokyo National Museum are published in the National Treasures of Japan series, edited by the Commission for Protection of Cultural Properties, vol. I. Tokyo, 1952. (The series is currently being printed.)
Numerous works are presented in:
Pageant of Japanese Art, edited by Staff Members of the Tokyo National Museum, 6 vols. Tokyo, 1952.
Art treasures of Japan, edited by Kokusai Bunka Shinkokai (Society for International Cultural Relations), 2 vols. Tokyo, 1960.

PERIODICALS

The museum publishes monographs on its own collections and two periodicals:
Tokyo Kokuritsu Hakubutsukan Kiyo (Proceedings of the Tokyo National Museum), vol. I. Tokyo, 1965.
Museum, Art Magazine edited by the Tokyo National Museum, vol. I. Tokyo, 1951.
(This monthly presents studies on unpublished works and summaries on new acquisitions.)
"Kokka" *and* "Bijutsu Kenkyu," *historical and critical magazines, also periodically publish articles on the museum's collections.*

INDEX OF ILLUSTRATIONS

INDEX OF NAMES

Note: The numbers in italics refer to names cited in the texts.

GENERAL INDEX